Some of Us Are Brave is a courageous exploration of Black feminism within the Black left, offering invaluable insights and igniting much-needed conversations. It is a must-read for anyone seeking a deeper understanding of this vital aspect of our history and the transformative power of Black feminist thought.

In a media landscape that often falls short when it comes to representing the voices of Black feminists, this series is a breath of fresh air.

> – Piper Carter
> Detroit-based Arts & Culture Organizer
> Host of "Beyond Breaking Barriers" podcast on Black Power Media

Reading Thandisizwe Chimurenga's third book, Some of Us are Brave: Interviews and Conversations with Sistas on Life, Art and Struggle – a compilation of interviews with a wide-range of Black women activists, scholars, and artists – is a bit like going to church; each chapter is akin to a great sermon delivered by a series of pastors, each more soul-stirring and enlightening than the last. It is a triumph of a book and I feel I am a better man for having read it.

> – Jon Jeter, author
> *Flat Broke in the Free Market: How Globalization Fleeced Working People,* former Washington Post foreign correspondent, former producer for *This American Life*

SOME OF US ARE BRAVE

Interviews and Conversations with Sistas on Life, Art and Struggle
2003–2017

Volume 2:
Black Lives Have Always Mattered
Black Women's Health
Bruthas on Sistas
Sistas in Struggle

Thandisizwe Chimurenga

Daraja Press

Published by
Daraja Press
https://darajapress.com
Wakefield, Quebec, Canada

© 2024 Thandisizwe Chimurenga
All rights reserved

Cover and interior design: Kate McDonnell
Printed and bound by CPI Group (UK) Ltd, Croydon, CR0 4YY
ISBN: 9781990263835

Library and Archives Canada Cataloguing in Publication

Title: Some of us are brave : interviews and conversations with sistas on life, art and struggle, 2003-2016 / Thandisizwe Chimurenga.

Names: Chimurenga, Thandisizwe, editor.

Description: Volume 2 has subtitle: Interviews and conversations with sistas on life, art and struggle, 2003-2017. | Includes bibliographical references. | Contents: Volume 2: Black lives have always mattered: black women's health, bruthas on sistas, sistas in struggle.

Identifiers: Canadiana 20230482341 | ISBN 9781990263835 (v.2 ; softcover)

Subjects: LCSH: Women, Black—United States—Interviews. | LCGFT: Interviews.

Classification: LCC HQ1163 .C45 2023 | DDC 305.48/896073—dc23

"'Tis woman's strongest vindication for speaking that the world needs to hear her voice. It would be subversive of every human interest that the cry of one-half the human family be stifled. ... The world has had to limp along with the wobbling gait and one-sided hesitancy of a man with one eye. Suddenly the bandage is removed from the other eye and the whole body is filled with light. It sees a circle where before it saw a segment. The darkened eye restored, every member rejoices with it."

– Anna Julia Cooper,
A Voice From the South, by a Black Woman of the South

It is the mission of SOUAB *(Some of Us Are Brave)* to provide an empowering space for women of Afrikan descent – to assist them in finding their voices and speaking their truths, their experiences and their perspectives to the world; to be a resource for the communities from which we come; and to make a contribution to the global movement for racial, economic, political and social justice and peace.

– Mission Statement, *Some of Us Are Brave*

vi

Table of contents

Preface by Shaunelle Curry vii
Introduction x
Acknowledgments xii

Black Lives Have Always Mattered

Assata Shakur 2
Elaine Brown 12
Ericka Huggins and Talibah Shakir 24
Geneva Reed-Veal 45
Honorable Cynthia McKinney 46
Janaya Khan 51
Kadiatou Diallo 63
Medusa 67
Michelle Alexander 69
Nisa Islam Muhammad 72
Patrisse Cullors 83
Ramona Africa 90
Sacajawea 'Saki' Hall 115
Samaria Rice 125

Black Women's Health

Byllye Avery and Iyanla Vanzant
On Forgiveness 128
Dorothy Roberts
Reproductive Justice 137
Nicole Sconiers
Black Women and Anxiety 143
PaSean Wilson
Black Women and Fibroids 148
The March for Women's Lives 154

Bruthas on Sistas

Clayton Lebouef
On Henrietta Vinton Davis 164

Gerald Horne
On Shirley Graham Du Bois 173

Robin Kelley
On Charlotta Bass... 177

Yusef Omowale
On Charlotta Bass... 179

Sistas in Struggle

Linda Evans
On Anti-Imperialism... 184

Stormy Ogden
On Indigenous Women in Prison 192

PREFACE
Shaunelle Curry

I met Thandisizwe Chimurenga in 2007 while I was working to shed light on the denigrating representation and invisibility of Black women and girls in the media through my initiative at the time, Mother's Day Radio (now Media Done Responsibly). "Shock Jock" Don Imus had called the Black Rutgers women's basketball players "nappy headed hoes" through his laughter on the national airwaves. Black women were gathered and fed up. We were angry and speaking out. In my work, I was calling for 24 hours of rest from misogynoir on the radio and 24 hours of music that honored Black women and girls with the visibility and respect our humanity required. I was honored to be interviewed by several activist journalists on KPFK in Los Angeles including Kelly Madison, Kali Alexander, Dedon Kimathi, and Thandi.

That Thandi – whew! There's nothing like being interviewed by Thandisizwe Chimurenga. The sound of her deep alto, borderline tenor resonant voice along with her not-to-be-messed-with demeanor was like a divining rod, pulling out the answers to her questions, sleuthing secrets you swore you'd never share. She is completely unphased by any cognitive dissonance you'll grapple with. Perhaps, you figure, she'll find the answers soon enough so you might as well go on and fess up now.

I learned that underneath that matter-of-fact journalistic tone is a heart of pure gold, a resounding laugh and tender smile, a deep love for Black folk, and an utter lack of tolerance for false narratives about Black women that feed patriarchy and racism while muffling our voices. Thandi's pen and mic are the great liberators of Black women's truths. She has mastered the art of listening, keying in on each detail and pinpointing the wisdom and experiences she wants to extract with her keen follow-up questions. "Excuse me, can we go back to what you said about..." She roots out the truth in plain language, in no-nonsense terms, and she requires the same from you.

That's exactly what Thandi offers here in Volume 2 of *Some of Us Are Brave*. I read this feeling like I was sitting at the kitchen table with the great Black women luminaries of activism telling it like it is, like they've seen it, felt it, heard it, tasted it, sweated it, sobbed it, laughed it, and embodied it. And I knew Thandi pulled out that divining rod on them with "one quick question, Sista," to which the reply would have been, "anything you need, Sis" and "I probably shouldn't be saying this," followed by them laying bare their souls.

And if she didn't interview them directly, she found the sources that did in raw impeccability, not spoon-fed for mainstream, but real and untempered for those who want the truth, nothing but that truth through the lens and voices of Black women. From activists to educators, to politicians and mamas of children slain by state violence, Thandi captures and collects their voices here for our consumption and care.

I am an educator, and still I gulped knowledge as if I'd been given entrance into a secret back room holding gems of wisdom most folk are denied. Through this anthology, I sat at tables with key members of the Black Panther Party of Self-Defense including Assata Shakur, Elaine Brown, Erika Huggins and Talibah Shakir. I witnessed the human in them, not the mystery or the mainstream myth. And in their stories, I saw mine. I was transported 30 years past their prime into my own, a 20-something moving through the ranks of Black liberation movements, finding my voice, locating my inner compass. I saw the foundation they laid through the transparency of their storytelling. I witnessed the challenges I thought were mine alone revealed through their organizational and self-critiques. I could relate to them as humans. I heard their inner thoughts and felt their fears, disillusionment, and courage well-up in me.

Each semester, at the start of my college courses on "race" and media, I point out to my students that none of us created racism, sexism, homophobia, or any of the oppressive institutionalized conditions that we were born into. But, we all inherited them and it is important to understand our place along the timeline of all things so we can know what has already been done, and what is left in our charge to do should we so choose. This is what Volume 2 of *Some of Us Are Brave* does for us. It plants us squarely in a timeline that reveals the radical work that has been done, the forces that would push up against that work, and the necessary coming together of our voices and collective power to create a world that works.

Prepare to grapple with cognitive dissonance of your own. You will not be spared Thandi's divining rod simply because you're a witness. Prepare to be challenged and learn something new whether you're reading this for credit in a college course or you're simply starved for knowledge of the inner workings and behind-the-scenes of those ongoing movements that work toward your liberation. And maybe you will learn like I have, that we're not doing anything new. We're carrying forward practices that are steeped in rich tradition. We are a part of this tradition, we are a part of this timeline. We are indeed, through this anthology, doing what Thandi commands - Sankofa. We're going back to fetch it, to learn from the brave and human who have tread this path, and we're creating a world that is better for what we've learned.

> – **Shaunelle Curry**
> Author, Shairi's Journey;
> Adjunct Professor, Department of TV, Film, Media and Pan-African Studies, Cal State LA;
> Founder, Media Done Responsibly

INTRODUCTION
Thandisizwe Chimurenga

Volume Two

Black Lives Have Always Mattered

Black Women's Health

Bruthas on Sistas

Sistas in Struggle

"Cuando una mujer negra habla, prest'atencion"
(When a Black woman speaks, pay attention.)

Volume One of *Some Of Us Are Brave* goes into better detail about how this work came into being. What I neglected to mention in Volume 1 is the history behind our name. Since we knew our purpose was to center the voices of Black women, I suggested to the group *When and Where We Enter*, from Paula Giddings' book on Black women's history here in the U.S., or *Some Of Us Are Brave* after the groundbreaking anthology on Black Women's Studies edited by Akasha Gloria Hull, Patricia Bell-Scott and Barbara Smith. The group chose the latter and we debuted on the airwaves of KPFK 90.7 FM as *Some Of Us Are Brave: A Black Womens' Radio Program* (SOUAB) on June 10, 2003.

These volumes exist as part of an effort to place intellectual production into our own Black hands and out of the hands of foundationally anti-Black institutions. It is but a small contribution to the literature on Black women's lives and thought primarily here in the United States. This documenting and preserving is a historical record and is proof that not only have we been here, we matter: to ourselves, our families, the communities from whence we come and the diaspora.

We tried to keep copies of every SOUAB program at the time that it aired. Sometimes we were successful or were able to get a copy at a later date, however, as a group, we never set up a centralized system or location for those copies. We never set up a de facto archive for SOUAB. Thus, this volume is made up primarily of my own work.

The majority of transcribed interviews/presentations contained here (Volume 2: Black Lives Have Always Mattered, Black Women's Health,

Introduction

Bruthas on Sistas and Sistas in Struggle, 2003-2017) were conducted and recorded by myself. They primarily aired on *Some of Us Are Brave* between 2003 and 2011. A few of the interviews and presentations transcribed here were recorded by me and aired elsewhere such as on *Beneath The Surface* or other programming on KPFK; the *Women's Magazine* on KPFA, the Pacifica sister station in Berkeley, California; WRFG community radio in Atlanta, Georgia; and one or two were planned to air and ended up gathering dust.

SOUAB started out as a one-hour show. Internal radio station chaos eventually cut the show to 30 minutes. This explains why some interviews are longer than others. There are also instances where I was simply getting "sound bites" from individuals and may or may not have interviewed them at a later date.

The interview with Patrice Cullors was conducted by me for a print outlet in 2015. The interview of Sacajawea "Saki" Hall was conducted in 2017 for inclusion in the book "Jackson Rising: The Struggle for Economic Democracy and Black Self-Determination in Jackson, Mississippi" published by Daraja Press.

Despite the absence of other Black women producers' work in this volume, trust me when I say that ALL who took the mic under the name of *Some of Us Are Brave* made a unique and great contribution to our world by amplifying the voices of Black women. *Asé!*

Thandisizwe Chimurenga
Los Angeles, CA
June 13, 2023

ACKNOWLEDGMENTS

The founders of *Some of Us Are Brave* are Ayanna Canada; Crystal Blackcreek Carlisle; J. Evan Dunlap; Iyatunde Folayan (Latrice Dixon); Grayce Gadsen; Sister Charlene Muhammad; Sherri Ross; Nancy Webb and myself; *Some of Us Are Brave* team members and supporters, at different times, were the following: Iyanifa Fayomi Falade Aworeni; Kali Sampson Alexander; Angela Birdsong; Laini Coffee; Rhonda Dixon; Jan Robinson Flint; Haleemah Henderson; Zakiya Kyle; Ellene Miles; Kaia Niambi Shivers, S. Pearl Sharp, and Oya Kali. All of you, every last one of you, made an invaluable contribution. I salute you.

To former KPFK management Eva Georgia (General Manager) Armando Gudino (Program Director) and Nate Scott (Operations Manager): Thank You for cracking that door open.

Many, Many Thanks and Tons of Love to Dave Adelson, Kwazi Nkrumah and my late but great compañero, Fernando Velasquez.

A *"Good Bruthas Lookin' Out For The Sistas"* Award goes to sound engineers Mark Maxwell and Teddy Robinson; Extra dap to Teddy for hookin' up such a dope theme; and ABSOLUTELY POSITIVELY NOTHING BUT LOVE to all KPFK Listeners and Guests for rocking with us for all those years. You are greatly appreciated.

To Christabel Nsiah-Buadi and Joanne Griffith: I should've taken your advice way, way earlier. Thank You.

Tatyanna Wilkinson and Angie Birdsong: y'all some hardcore MVPs. Love You! Thank You!

To Nana Gyamfi and Dr. Karin L. Stanford, my sistas from other misters: Medase for your SistaShip;

Huge Thanks to the initial funders to get transcripts for this book: Baba Kofi Opantiri (Rest In Eternal Peace)| Maryanne | Carlos | Merna | Michael | Dez | Frieda and Katherine | Sheba | Baye | Dorothy | Casey | Pamela | Ginna | Charles | Kali | Mama Geri | Zenzele | Jennifer | Lorelei | Lynn | Chris | Shawn | Yvette | and Makani

Big, Huge, Ginormous Thanks to Jesse Strauss, Frieda Werden and Makani Themba: your assistance with transcription has to be really, really shouted out. Like, REALLY.

Acknowledgments

To Firoze Manji and the staff and comrades of Daraja Press: thank you for your enthusiasm, your support and most of all your patience. *Nakupenda!*

Lastly, but most importantly, I thank Almighty Mother-Father God, my Ancestors and the Orishas/Obosum who continue to hold me up, and my brother Darryl and sister-in-law Miriam for their material support of my work. Love You! Thank You!

Inevitably, unfortunately, someone is always left out of an acknowledgment. Please charge it to my head and not my heart.

Thandi

Black Lives
Have Always Mattered

Assata Shakur

This recording aired sometime in 2004 on "The Liberation Hour" on KPFK, a temporary Wednesday evening program that would eventually move to Saturdays under the name of "Feedom Now," hosted by Dedon Kamathi.

Thandisizwe Chimurenga: *We'll consider the future of our movements for self-determination and liberation by looking back to 1993, where tonight we will hear excerpts of a critical conversation with Assata Shakur in Havana, Cuba.*

Assata Shakur, former member of the Black Panther Party and reputed member of the Black Liberation Army, was falsely accused and wrongly sentenced to prison in the mid-1970s on various bank robbery charges.

On November 2, 1979, she was liberated from the Clinton Correctional Facility for Women in New Jersey and later was given political asylum in the revolutionary state of Cuba. In 1993, a delegation from the New African Women's Task Force, a unit of the New Afrikan People's Organisation, traveled to Cuba to dialogue honestly and critically with this revolutionary sister about her experiences with sexism and patriarchy in the movement, and to discuss strategies to combat this evil.

The spirit of Sankofa[1] says that in order to move forward, we must look back. There's no shame in going back and being critical, analytical, looking

---

1 Sankofa is a word from the Akan language of Ghana that means "go back and get it." It is often used to refer to a cultural concept and practice that encourages people to look back to their cultural heritage in order to move forward and build a better future. Sankofa is often used as a symbol of African-American cultural heritage and is used in a wide range of contexts, from art and fashion to education and activism.

at things with new and fresh eyes in order to step with a sure footing into the future. Our movements for freedom, for reparations, for liberation, for independence, for social justice, do not have any place in them for homophobia or for sexism. Homophobia and sexism are the twin sons of patriarchy. In the Black community, we have yet to have discussions on these topics in an honest and frank manner in which everyone can say what's on their mind.

Our first presentation, as I stated earlier, is an excerpt from a critical conversation with Assata Shakur in Havana, Cuba. This presentation was given to the New African Women's Task Force, which is a unit of the New Afrikan People's Organisation. In this talk, Sister Assata talks frankly about experiences that she and other women had in various movements for liberation, and she gives her ideas on strategies to combat certain evils that we face. In the beginning, she was asked, because she is considered to be a leader in our struggle, what were her thoughts?

• • •

Assata Shakur: You know what, I really don't see myself as an important leader, I see myself as a woman who is committed to social change. It's important to make that distinction because when you start seeing yourself as an important leader, you start getting crazy [laughs] ... Your question is an important one because the question of sexism affects political work in many senses. For example, I joined the movement in the 1960s and I participated in different organizations. Since I was new and young and didn't know anything, I basically was happy being a "gopher"[2] because you can learn a lot being a gopher. I didn't want to spend the rest of my life as a gopher. And there came a time when I began to resent, people thinking that it was my biological destiny to be a gopher. That's when it started to get rough. [Laughter] And I began to see that the sisters were the most efficient people in almost all of the organizations that I worked with; were also the most silent people in all of the organizations that I worked with; were also the most neglected, unlistened to group of people in all of the organizations that I worked with. And were also the most powerless people in all the organizations I worked with, and the image of a leader was always male. When people would talk about leadership, they called the leader "he." There was never any female counterpart of the leader.

---
2 'go for' – go for this this, go for that.

After being in the movement for a while, I got categorized as an animal called a "good sister" or a "strong sister." Now a good sister, a strong sister, is supposed to work like a horse from morning to night, cover everybody's mistakes, "Oh, I need this tomorrow." So you sit up all night typing and neglect other parts of your life that are really necessary, that are really important, to cover some inefficient, unprincipled mistake or negligent part on the part of your male comrades.

Going through that many times, sometimes it would really make me angry because I would often sit up and say, "We need a statement about something, something, something." When you could write, everybody wants you to write, so you sit down and you're the writer. I'd sit up all night, and I'd go the next day to the meeting and nobody would show. I'd say, "Well, what happened?" "Oh didn't you know the meeting was canceled?" I went through literally years of that on all different kinds of levels.

I was very committed so it was very difficult for me to say no. It was very difficult for me to get into personal things like, "Well, you didn't do what you were supposed to do, never blah blah blah." Because it was just a hassle, I didn't want to be bothered, and it wasn't until later, that I knew that it wasn't a personal hassle, that it was something that I had to address on a principled level.

The abuse of the work, not only my work but the abuse of sisters' work, the ignoring. You could say something, and you'd be talking for 15 minutes and then people say "mmhmm," and then some brother would get up and repeat something that you said, and they say, "That's a good idea, brother!" You know? What is this? What am I dealing with? What do I have to do? Who do I have to be, to be respected, to be listened to? What must I be to be a comrade?

It's a struggle. It's something that we all as women have to face: how do we make ourselves heard? As I was telling some of you yesterday, you just could not be the human being that you were. I couldn't be who I was because I'm like a little timid. There's this image but I am naturally timid, naturally shy ... to get in front of a group of people, the first time I had to do it, I thought I was just going to literally die right then and there, because I had been socialized to be timid.

It wasn't just that my personality was timid but it was the way that I had been socialized, women weren't supposed to get up in front of crowds of women. That was not an image that came easily to you, that was not something that I was crying for. So it was like, "Oh, my God." I had to overcome that, and so that when you see strong women who hold strong positions in revolutionary struggles, you know what they went through. It wasn't just that they didn't go through what men went through. Men go through half of what women go through to become effective political leaders. Because it's easy for them, it's easy for their work to be recognized because other men are anxious to recognize their work. When I started becoming active in political organizations, men were not anxious to recognize my work, they were anxious to recognize my body.

And it was always very difficult for me to get past the body trick. I mean, to really get around it because it always came up. It came up in that I would have problems with people because they wanted to get in my draws and then once it was clear there wasn't nothing happening, then I was on their shit list for the rest of the duration. Then if you had a relationship with somebody and then it was over, it was like this whole attitude of, "well we relate personally." Well, wait a minute, this is a political issue; our relationship has nothing to do with this, never did and never will. We're talking about apples and you talking about peaches. What is the point? Women are constantly confronted with these issues in our political work. And if we don't say, "Look, these are the ethical ways that the sexes have to work together." Other things are not just personal things, but they are politically unethical. And, for example ... we were brainwashed, there is no question about it because part of the whole psychology of women, is you are not educated to be the leader, but you are educated to go to bed with the leader, to fall in love with the leader. The leader is your hero. Everybody is trying to get next to him this way, and that way. There was a lot of that going on in all of us mentally. We were at a serious disadvantage in our relationships with men because we were very confused about what we wanted also.

It wasn't a question of just the men. It was a question of us too because we accepted a lot of things that were clearly unprincipled because we were trying to get next to some dude. It was part of our psychology. But, you know, part of it was also the 1960s. When I look back on it … I don't think that I was to the same kind of vibe that Elaine Brown described as being free love, et cetera. But I feel regret that I did not take some of those relationships that I made more seriously.

Part of it was my childhood, just being young. Another part of it was that I had not reached the kind of consciousness that I have now that … political struggle is not just about changing structures. It's not enough to talk about "I want to change a government," it's not enough to talk about "a chicken in every pot" or "democracy" or whatever. You have to internalize it. That means changing your relationships with other human beings, changing your ability to care about other human beings. And one of the things that I see now is we have a very totally male-dominated political structure, a political style, a political way of working, but we also had a very male-oriented way of relating to each other on a whole series of levels.

For example, women: if you had PMS – and nobody had heard of it then – it was your problem. Who cares if you have cramps? Ain't nobody worried about your cramps. Don't nobody here want to hear about your baby. Don't nobody want to hear about your babysitters or your lack of babysitters or anything else. You are supposed to be at the meeting. Nobody is concerned about … what? Dinner? Where does it come from? It's supposed to come from you and if it doesn't come from you then you know you've got to fight not to be in the kitchen. I remember people trying to herd me into the kitchen … honey, you are herding the wrong person in the kitchen. I'll go in that kitchen, and what you got … I can't cook! You better herd somebody else!

For years I wouldn't cook and that was just my self-defense against somebody trying to herd me into the kitchen because we had this liberation school, right? I was in college and all of a sudden nobody even thought of it. All the directors of the school were men. We are all students the same year, but all the directors were men. Then came lunch, you had to feed the kids, "All right sisters. Will the sisters go to the kitchen and prepare the food?"

I'm trying to teach kids 13, 14 years old, they can barely read, multiply, divide. Okay, I'm committed to this. You know I'm going to get these kids somewhere this summer, we are going to work. Then in the afternoon, I got arts and crafts up to my head in paint, and everything else. Somebody wants me to go in the middle of this and cook lunch? Are you crazy?

So finally, after a big struggle the food came from somewhere else and brothers helped or whatever, but it got resolved, but the immediate idea, in the 1960s, was who would do it. "What's the problem? You don't like to cook, don't you know you are a woman?" Being an African woman added a whole extra level, because you were supposed to be like your sisters in Africa and the reason why everything was so messed up was because the African family had gone astray, because we had castrated our men … "We did castrate our men." I was like, "Oh, my God did I do that?" [laughter]

Yes, but there was a whole thing about Black women as castrators. I would go to meetings, I mean this is in the early 1960s. Brothers would seriously propose that sisters should walk 10 feet behind the brothers. It would be serious proposals. They would get up and they run this stuff and you'd be like "HUH?" Then the next thing was like, "You must bring a bowl." We do this cultural event and the sisters was supposed to bring this bowl with the water so that the brothers could wash their hands and stuff. There were organizations at that time, where sisters were supposed to bend their heads down when brothers came in. And I don't want to mention any names of organizations, but there is enough sisters around that if we ever get to tell our stories in the movement, it would be a very interesting project, in terms of a book or in terms of a film, because the experiences were devastating. They were devastating to many women, because a lot of women were serious about struggling and then got into the struggle, got into a relationship, and were totally frustrated in their ability to struggle, because of personal resistance from their mates, from their organization, and had no backup.

[Break]

TC: And we are Black on *The Liberation Hour* with music by Angelique Kidjo[3] and Assata Shakur, former member of the Black Panther Party and the Black Liberation Army. Speaking to a delegation of the New Afrikan Women's Taskforce in Havana Cuba, in 1993 about her experiences in the movement. We continue now with the dialogue. Sister Assata was asked,

---

3 Angélique Kidjo (born 1960) is a Beninese-French singer-songwriter, actress, and activist who has won five Grammy awards. In 2007, *Time* magazine called her "Africa's premier diva."

"What are some of the things that we can do to combat most of the ills she talked about?"

Sanovia Muhammad, New Afrikan Women's Taskforce: So how do you ... what's the direction or guidelines in terms of where we are today?

AS: I think the first step toward changing things is to educate. And I think that the first people that we have to educate are ourselves. I think that we have to go through and identify the different things that as political activists, women suffer; the different things that women in our communities suffer. To start addressing those things, systematically, bit by bit.

So we need an analysis; if you don't have an analysis of the problem it's very difficult to educate. So the first thing for us to do is to make an analysis of where we are. We've made some progress. Sisters are much more aware, thank goodness, than we were 10, 20 years ago. And we've got to start sharing that with each other, sharing that with younger sisters, writing about it, documenting what our struggle has been and then, trying to take it to another level.

One of the problems that we have is being unorganized. There are a lot of ways that sisters can be organized ... we can be organized in political organizations, and you are all in a taskforce and I think that's very important, but it's a lot of survival organizing that we can do, we can get together in terms of childcare collectives, whether it's in terms of healing collectives, whether its in terms ... and by healing collectives, I've heard some very positive things about healing collectives and some very negative things that, "come tell all and touchy feely and cry all day." I'm not talking about that. When I talk about healing collectives, I think it's important for us to get things that are in our systems out and some of the pain out, but I think that it's also ... that's useless unless we do something. I think that a lot of healing has to do with activity, because otherwise what's the point? Is heal to do what? Stay a victim? To damn your daughters to the same situation that you're in? So if you're not actively doing something then I think that, in terms of changing reality, then the whole "healing approach" thing is fraudulent.

When I say doing something, I don't mean any specific thing. Writing is doing something; speaking is doing something; there are all kinds of ways of activity and I don't believe that there's any one way that people need to act nor do I believe there's any one way that people need to organize. I think that in terms of pure survival, I think sisters need to organize collectives to support sisters who are homeless and to support each other in those kinds of things. I think that, whether it's in terms of jobless sisters or ... I mean there's so many ways that we can organize that we don't. I think we just need to just analyze where we are and what would we do to reach out to other sisters.

I think that it's important in order for us to be able to effectively reach out to other sisters to really struggle within our own movement against homophobia, because I think that one of the things that has held us back in terms of sisters reaching out to sisters has been the issue of homophobia.

Because, you know, you take a sister from one movement and she goes to a meeting and they're 30 lesbians in the meeting. Now, she has no prior experience with lesbians and no clear political position about lesbians, then she gets freaked out, and then there's the whole thing of, "I don't want anybody to think I'm a lesbian" and all this stuff. But I think that if you really are serious about dealing with the issue of struggling against homophobia, that you have to deal with that and not permit any sister to be, for lack of another word, "gay baited."

Because somebody asked me if I'm gay, so what if I am? What is your point in asking me? You asking that, to ask what? What does that have to do with the time of day? Do you wanna go out? You know what I mean? ... And I don't allow people to play those kinds of games with me because I don't like those kinds of games. I think that it's difficult at first, but I think as one's principles become stronger, then, you know, I don't feel any need to argue with anybody about anything, I'm not really concerned. Sometimes, I've been in a situation and because I'm always alone or ... someone [will say] "she's gay," and I have been thankful! It has been ... so much easier to work ... "keep thinkin' [that]! Fine!" I enjoy the distance, to tell you the truth, at different times and places because, you know, men somehow they treat you in another way. I have not found those kinds of things to be a problem once I decided where my politics were, where my sentiments were and who I am, and have no problem being myself.

I think that we're at a point now that we have so many problems as a people that we have to really define what morality is and isn't. I think that we all grew up being exposed to a kind of homophobic morality and people said that "if a man doesn't go to bed with another man and a woman doesn't go to bed with another woman and you have sex after you're married and not before, then, you're moral." Now, as far as I'm concerned, that is the kind of morality that the right wing is trying to push. And if we have the same morality, then we fall into a whole lot of tracks.

Because what happens is they can talk about who's going to bed with who, who isn't and who is, and that's moral but they could be all around the world, all around the country, oppressing people, beating people to death, burning crosses, saying "I'm moral." I think that is a totally reactionary type of morality, and for people who really are interested in social change, we have to really cover what is moral.

[Break]

TC: You are listening to excerpts of a conversation with sister Assata Shakur, former member of the Black Panther Party and the Black Liberation Army in Havana, Cuba in 1993. She was speaking with a delegation of women from the New Afrikan Women's Task Force regarding her experiences dealing in the movement, our movements for liberation. In this final brief segment, she was asked about the issue of violence against women.

AS: The United States is so violent in all aspects that violence against women would inevitably increase. The culture makes everybody more violent, and one of the most unfortunate things is its effect on women because we're seen as easy targets. We're not supposed to be able to fight, we're not supposed to be able to defend ourselves, so every man thinks of us as, "I can beat her." They don't even think about the possibility that you might be able to beat them. Which really makes them easily beatable, because if you know a little something, you can kick their ass.

We're also very much brainwashed into thinking that the men can beat us up. Even though they are stronger physically, but when it comes to fighting, physical strength without discipline without knowledge is of very little use. So that I think that sisters need to get a whole 'nother consciousness about our bodies, about who we are, and what we're capable of doing. Because, in a fight, the most important thing is not to panic; to be able to think, to be able to calculate, to be able to figure out "what's the next move?" And in most things, we are better at doing that in most every category than men are. Then that should make us naturally very good warriors. In African tradition, from thousands of years ago, sisters have been warriors and bodyguards. And so I think that we have been very much brainwashed as a result of our experience on the plantation, the new plantation and the old one, about who we are and about what we're capable of. So I think one of the things that we've got to do as sisters is start talking to other sisters about our body power and really forming a culture of body awareness among ourselves.

Elaine Brown

Elaine Brown is a former member, Minister of Information and Chair of the Black Panther Party for Self Defense (BPP). The first and only woman ever to lead the Party, she also ran for the Oakland (California) City Council through the BPP. She remains active today in developing cooperative economic ventures in partnership with formerly incarcerated persons.

This recording aired sometime in 2004 on "The Liberation Hour" on KPFK, a temporary Wednesday evening program that would eventually move to Saturdays under the name of "Freedom Now," hosted by Dedon Kamathi.

• • •

Elaine Brown: I want to start out by saying – we used to say back in the day – I've got fifteen to twenty minutes and I'm gonna use all twenty; cause you can't cover the whole history of the Black Panther Party or anything like that, or talk about today's issues in a very little time, and then we will have question and answer.

I want to start out by saying what we used to say in the Black Panther Party, and that is: power to the people. All power to the people.

That's what we were talking about; and I don't just mean a few of us – I mean all of us. And I mean all of us together, not a few of us who are here, but all of our people who are not here.

I want to say something about the history of the Black Panther Party, but I do want to mention that I was the Chairman of the Black Panther Party, not to be confused with the Chairperson or the Chair, because we really didn't chair. The office was called "Chairman" so that's the office I took over. So that's the name. My title was "Chairman of the Black Panther Party," and I want to mention briefly, that a lot of people wonder: "How did you get to be the Chairman of the Black Panther Party?" and there are people who have asked me many times if I rose through the ranks as though there was some sort of corporate board, and I got elected to the Chairmanship of the corporation. And people thought, said, "Did you sleep your way to the top?" Yes. And I was accused at one time of having slept with Bunchy Carter.[1] Some guy asked: "I heard you slept with Bunchy Carter, with Eldridge Cleaver,[2] with Huey Newton,[3] and that's how you got to be the Chairman of the Black Panther Party. What do you say to that?"

The first thing I say is I never slept with Bunchy Carter. [chuckle] And the second thing I would say, you don't know who he is, but suffice it to say he is well-known among the ranks of the Black Panther Party. The second thing I would say is that Eldridge Cleaver slept with half of the women in the State of California in and out of the Black Panther Party at the time. And the third thing is that Huey Newton surely slept with the other half, okay? And none of those women became Chairman of the Black Panther Party. So ...

[applause]

So what can we conclude about that? And what we might conclude is that either that was not the criterion for becoming Chairman of the Black Panther Party [pause/chuckles] or I must've had the baddest pussy in the State of California!

[wild applause]

You always have to answer an absurd question with an absurd answer, 'cause too many women start defending themselves, how they did this and how they did ... STOP. You know? Let's take it there. Now let's talk about

---

1 Alprentice "Bunchy" Carter (1942-1969) was a founding member of the Southern California chapter of the Black Panther Party. Carter was shot and killed in 1969.
2 Eldridge Cleaver (1935-1998) was an American writer and political activist who became an early leader of the Black Panther Party. Much later, he became a Mormon and a Republican.
3 Huey Newton (1942-1989) was an American activist and revolutionary who co-founded the Black Panther Party for Self Defense (BPP) in 1966 with Bobby Seale. The party was initially focused on armed self-defense against police brutality and oppression of Black people.

the Black Panther Party, because I know a lot of you heard of the Party, but most people know very little because the American public school system is not gonna teach you anything. It takes a lot to root out that information, find information, about these organizations, and really have a sense. And since we're not dead yet – Kathy and Heather, thank goodness I suppose – we're not yet dead yet, what we get to do is tell the story.

And so let me just say something about the Black Panther Party, because it has to be contextualized as a part of the continuation of the Black struggle for freedom from the time of the Emancipation Proclamation.[4] Because Black people, of course, in 1865 after the end of the Civil War and Lincoln allegedly freed the slaves, and all that mythical history that we read in our history books; when the 13th amendment[5] was passed before it was even ratified in the South where the majority of Black people live, you had something passed – a series of laws passed – that can collectively be called the Black Codes.[6] The Black Codes regulated the behavior of Blacks and primarily criminalized Blacks for being "vagrant." That is to say, if you didn't have a job you could go to jail. Sounds almost like today, doesn't it?

So we have the Black Codes and the criminalization of Black people at the time, the same time we had the rise of the KKK[7] and other white terrorist organizations. At the same time, we had the failure of the 40 acres plan. The 40 acres plan of course was to do what? To provide every former slave family 40 acres of land to get started after 250 years as slaves – not just as slaves but as property. Not just as property, but as having no relevance to the society at all, being called by Jefferson: "An inferior people"; being told by the

---

4 The Emancipation Proclamation was an executive order issued by U.S. President Abraham Lincoln on January 1, 1863, during the American Civil War (1861-1865). The Proclamation changed the legal status of more than 3.5 million enslaved African-Americans in the secessionist Confederate states from enslaved to free.
5 The Thirteenth Amendment to the U.S. Constitution abolished slavery and involuntary servitude, except as punishment for a crime. The amendment was ratified by the required 27 of the then 36 states on December 6, 1865, and proclaimed on December 18. It was the first of the three Reconstruction Amendments adopted following the American Civil War.
6 The Black Codes were laws which governed the conduct of African-Americans (both free and freed Black people). The best known of these laws were passed by Southern states in 1865 and 1866, after the Civil War, in order to restrict African Americans' freedom, and in order to compel them to work for either low or no wages.
7 The Ku Klux Klan, often called the KKK, is an American white supremacist group whose primary targets are African-Americans, Hispanics, Jews, Latinos, Asian Americans, Native Americans, and Catholics, as well as immigrants, leftists, homosexuals, Muslims, atheists and abortion providers. The first Klan was established in the wake of the American Civil War. It sought to overthrow the Republican state governments in the South, especially by using voter intimidation and targeted violence against African-American leaders. The KKK is still very much alive in the United States.

Jacksonians that America was a white Anglo-protestant-Saxon country and that Blacks really had no place to be in. Lincoln himself saying that he always knew that the white race was superior, no matter whatever the emancipation proclamation said about freeing the slaves in the seceding states.

Now I mention this history because if you don't contextualize it, then you start thinking of some sort of romantic imagery of the Black Panther Party, and not seeing it in its context. You had in 1896, what? You had the Supreme Court ruling in, what? Plessy. Plessy v Ferguson[8] was the story of Homer Plessy – a light-skinned Black who tried to get on a train in Louisiana, and Louisiana law said it was segregated trains. Plessy first said he wasn't really that Black. That was his first argument to the Supreme Court – "I shouldn't even be categorized as Black, I'm an octoroon."[9] That's how sad the story is in this world. And then went on to say: "if I am Black, then I have the right as a citizen to sit on the same car with whites." And the court said: "Well, here's the thing. We can't regulate social arrangements, so your citizenship priorities do not extend to private enterprise. So we'll say: as long as you have equal accommodations they can be separate."

And of course, that was the beginning of what? American apartheid.[10] Hmm?

Now, if you don't know that – that's 1896. So that's just a little over 100 years ago, and the rest of the story is fighting how to survive in a land of Plessy without 40 acres and being criminalized under Black Codes and so-forth and so-on. And so we have a struggle that took place, at the same time the influx of European immigrants coming in – you know, "Give me your tired, your poor," so they can be exploited as workers in industrial worker fields. And so, keep the Blacks out of industry because America is basically through with Blacks – we had already grown all the cotton so that America

---

8 Plessy v. Ferguson was a landmark U.S. Supreme Court decision which ruled that racial segregation laws did not violate the U.S. Constitution as long as the facilities for each race were equal in quality, a doctrine that came to be known as "separate but equal".
9 Octoroon: In the U.S., a quadroon was a person with one quarter African and three quarters European ancestry, while an octoroon was one-eighth Black. The U.S. adhered to the "one drop rule" which said that any person with even one Black ancestor is considered Black.
10 Apartheid was a system of institutionalized racial segregation that existed in South Africa and South West Africa (now Namibia) from 1948 to the early 1990s. Apartheid ensured that South Africa was dominated politically, socially and economically by the nation's dominant minority white population. Apartheid legislation was repealed on 17 June 1991, leading to multiracial elections in April 1994.

was the biggest producer of cotton in the world. We had already picked all the rice or developed all the rice, and been through all the rice paddies that made South Carolina the largest producer of rice, and so forth.

So now America was finished. The steam engine was here. It was time to roll west and kill some more native people and get started on a new wave of industrialization, and we now are in the new wave of what? Technological advance.

So at that pivotal moment, Blacks really had no role to play – poor Europeans coming in under contract work, and so on and so forth. So here we were, babbling not for freedom of the press or any of these abstract, nebulous freedoms that we can't really eat or live by, but for survival, for food, for housing, for jobs, for healthcare, and for those things that you need just to get through the day. Okay?

And so what Black people did... Booker T. Washington[11] led the call that said: "Look. We're not going to try to integrate into your society. We will be like 5 fingers on a hand. For all things economic we will be as one, but for social things we will be separate because we really not tryna marry your daughters, we're just tryna survive. So we will stay where we are."

A lot of people thought Booker T. Washington was a reactionary because he's been revisited and revisited, but the bottom line was this was a way for former slaves to try to figure out: how are we going to survive in a hostile, hostile strange land?

Then of course you had the Du Bois[12] tendency coming in at the turn of the century talking about integration into America, and then you had Marcus Garvey[13] following up on the program of Booker T. Washington, talking about economic independence for Blacks, and so forth.

---

11 Booker T. Washington (1856-1915) was an American educator, author and orator. Between 1890 and 1915, Washington was the dominant leader in the African-American community. As lynchings in the South reached a peak in 1895, Washington gave a speech, known as the "Atlanta compromise", that called for Black progress through education and entrepreneurship, rather than trying to challenge Jim Crow segregation and disenfranchisement of Black voters in the South. William Monroe Trotter and W. E. B. Du Bois were among Black opponents of Washington's compromise.

12 W.E.B. Du Bois (1868-1963) was a sociologist, historian, civil rights activist, and writer. He was the first African-American to earn a PhD from Harvard University. Du Bois co-founded the National Association for the Advancement of Colored People (NAACP) and authored many works, including *The Souls of Black Folk* and *Black Reconstruction in America*. He died in Ghana after the United States refused to renew his passport.

13 Marcus Garvey (1887-1940) was a Jamaican political activist, publisher, journalist and orator. He was the founder of the Universal Negro Improvement Association (UNIA). Garvey campaigned for an end to European colonial rule across Africa and advocated the political unification of the continent.

Now, why am I just talking about Black people, especially in a room predominated by whites? And you have to acknowledge these differences because if you don't acknowledge them and act like they don't matter, then you don't get what the drill is here. And the drill is that the destiny of Black people in America is absolutely tied to the destiny of white people in America. You cannot have a completely oppressed, large percentage of people pretend that you have a free country, okay?

So our destinies are all tied together now.

So here comes Marcus Garvey talking about economic independence for Blacks, and of course J Edgar Hoover[14]– little J Edgar Hoover – was already on the scene, gettin' ready to destroy folks from the get-go in the 1920s, late 1920s, oust Marcus Garvey from the United States and so forth. And then we have a situation where Blacks began to do all kinds of things to develop different programs and campaigns about – "don't shop where you can't work," anti-lynching campaigns, and so-forth. These were all survival measures that were taking place at the beginning of the turn of the century, in the 1910s, the '20s, the '30s and so forth and so on.

And so we get to that great vote in 1954, when little Linda Brown tries to go to school in Topeka, Kansas, and says: "Look, I'm tired of walking four miles down the road to a burnt down, degraded school. I would like to come to school right across the street here." And the NAACP takes the case to the Supreme Court, and we get the decision in Brown,[15] and what does Brown say? It says: we overturn Plessy as to public education, and we're saying that separate is not equal in public education. We call for the desegregation of American schools.

Now, do we know of any battle that got more ugly than it did when white people in America found out that their children would have to sit in a public school with Black children, than that? And it wasn't just of course in Mississippi, it was in Massachusetts. And it was everywhere throughout America, we had bloodshed over the simple question of the desegregation

---

14 J. Edgar Hoover (1895-1972) served as the first Director of the FBI from 1935 until his death in 1972. Hoover is remembered for his often controversial tactics and methods, and his powerful influence over American law enforcement and politics during his time in office.

15 Brown v. Board of Education of Topeka was a landmark decision by the U.S. Supreme Court which ruled that state laws establishing racial segregation in public schools are unconstitutional, even if the segregated schools are otherwise equal in quality. The decision partially overruled the Court's 1896 decision Plessy v. Ferguson.

of schools. Of course today, we realize that schools have been completely resegregated. Not that it matters, because schools aren't teaching very much to anybody anyway, but, nevertheless, they are segregated.

[Applause]

1955 we have, of course, that moment that Rosa Parks,[16] like Plessy sixty-some years before, tried to get on a bus in Montgomery, said she wasn't going to give up her seat to anybody. Can you imagine that from 1865, here we are in 1955, trying to talk about just getting a seat on a bus. We're not even talking about 40 acres. We're not talking about food, we're not talking about housing, we're not talking about healthcare. We're talking about just getting a seat on a bus.

And of course, this gave rise to what we now can think of as the Civil Rights Movement, with Dr. King[17] leading and giving moral voice to why America had to change and be turned around. And of course, given the rise of television and so forth, everybody around the world was now seeing America and the dogs – all the pictures that we now see 'cause that's how we think the Civil Rights Movement rises. Various organizations and people: You've got Ella Baker[18] – a book's coming out with some information about her. Ella Baker, people like Ella Baker, and the SNCC[19] people and all these various organizations of Freedom Riders.[20] And eventually there was a call for Black Power, and nobody really knew what it meant, but all of us who were Black kinda liked that. We liked what it was. We didn't know what it was, but we wanted it. Said we wanted some power, we wanted to be Black too.

---

16 Rosa Parks (1913-2005) was an activist in the American civil rights movement. Her refusal to give up her bus seat to a white passenger sparked the Montgomery, Alabama bus boycott and ultimately led to a Supreme Court decision declaring that segregation on public transportation was unconstitutional.
17 Martin Luther King Jr. (1929-1968) was an American Baptist minister and activist who was one of the most prominent leaders in the civil rights movement from 1955 until his assassination in 1968.
18 Ella Baker (1903-1986) was an African-American civil rights and human rights activist. She was a largely behind-the-scenes organizer whose career spanned more than five decades. She promoted grassroots organizing, radical democracy, and the ability of the oppressed to understand their worlds and advocate for themselves.
19 The Student Nonviolent Coordinating Committee (SNCC) was the principal channel of student commitment in the United States to the civil rights movement during the 1960s. Emerging in 1960 from the student-led sit-ins at segregated lunch counters in Greensboro, North Carolina, and Nashville, Tennessee, the Committee challenged the civic segregation and political exclusion of African-Americans. Following an aborted merger with the Black Panther Party in 1968, SNCC effectively dissolved.
20 Freedom Riders were civil rights activists who rode interstate buses into the segregated Southern United States starting in 1961 to challenge the non-enforcement of two U.S. Supreme Court decisions which ruled that segregated public buses were unconstitutional.

You know, in the same time, we had the 1963 march on Washington[21], and we had the 1964 Civil Rights Bill passed around the same time as Watts was burning[22] and as Johnson[23] was invading the Gulf of Tonkin.[24] And you had a bunch of people running around the world – running around this country – talkin' 'bout "we don't want to have no more war," and those voices included not only Martin Luther King, one of the few Blacks who was actually calling for an end to the war in Vietnam, and was denounced by a lot of the other moderate Blacks and other Blacks. And the Black Panther Party coming to being in 1966.

And what was the Black Panther Party? The Black Panther Party also came out of that whole notion of Black Power, but we were talking about Black liberation. And what did we mean by that? We identified that in a ten-point platform or program. We said in essence we wanted food, clothing, housing, justice, education, peace, land. These were the things that we wanted – very concrete, not an abstract struggle, but a very concrete struggle.

But we said: "How can we talk about the liberation of Black people in the face of the complete oppression and almost the murder – complete genocide – of the indigenous people? We said we couldn't do it?" We couldn't talk about our freedom in the context of the oppression of native people, and so we helped to form a kind of coalition with the American Indian Movement. Leonard Peltier is still in prison today behind the activities of AIM. So how could we be free when the Mexican, Xicanos, were picking all that food in California and entire countries eating that food – if you're vegetarian you're still eating that food and it's still getting picked by exploited workers, so don't get excited about yourself.

[Laughter, applause]

We said we cannot be free as long as the Xicano population in California and elsewhere were exploited, so we helped to form a coalition with the

---

21 The March on Washington was held in Washington, D.C., on August 28, 1963. The purpose of the march was to advocate for the civil and economic rights of African Americans. At the march, Dr. Martin Luther King Jr. delivered his historic "I Have a Dream" speech in which he called for an end to racism.
22 The Watts riots took place in the Watts neighborhood of Los Angeles from August 11-16, 1965 in response to police abuse against African-Americans. Six days of civil unrest resulted in 34 deaths as well as over $40 million in property damage.
23 Lyndon Baines Johnson (1908-1973) served as the president of the United States from 1963 to 1969.
24 The Gulf of Tonkin incident in August 1964 was an international confrontation that led to the United States engaging more directly in the Vietnam War.

Brown Berets. How could we talk about freedom in America when the Puerto Rican workers in the industrial fields of New York can't find any kind of freedom? We can't be, so we helped to form or formed a coalition with the Young Lords. How can we be free when poor white people in Appalachia and elsewhere cannot get jobs and can't even get running water in many cases? So we helped to form a coalition with and formed the Patriot Party coming out of Chicago. We already had coalitions with the Peace and Freedom Party, with Students for a Democratic Society, and ultimately with the Weather Underground and so forth.

And so we talked about coalition building, and said, well, wait a minute. How can we be free when half the country is oppressed? And we were the only Black organization to call for women's liberation as a part of the liberation of Black people. How could we be free when gays are oppressed in America? Matter of fact, Huey Newton issued one of the first statements about gay liberation, and said: "Perhaps the homosexual is the most oppressed person in America." So we formed coalitions with gay liberation organizations. How can we be free when people who are handicapped, with wheelchairs, can't even have access to the most minimal kinds of independence as human beings? So we formed a coalition with the Center for Independent Living and helped to tear down some of these walls so that people could do that. How could we talk about our freedom when the environment is polluted? So we talked about forming coalitions with the Trust for Public Land and other environmental groups. How could we talk about freedom in America when the Vietnamese are oppressed by these very same people? So we supported the Viet Cong,[25] and matter of fact, we called a victory for the Vietnamese. How could we talk about our freedom when the people of South Africa are not free? So we formed a coalition with the PAC (Pan Africanist Congress of Azania). What about in Mozambique? Formed a coalition with FRELIMO[26]. What about in Cuba? Formed a partnership with Cubans. What about China? What about the world? We became

---

25 The Viet Cong was a guerrilla force that fought against the United States and South Vietnam during the Vietnam War. The name "Viet Cong" was a shortened version of "Vietnamese Communists": the group was made up of members of the Communist Party of Vietnam, as well as other communist and nationalist groups. The Viet Cong officially disbanded after the end of the Vietnam War in 1975.

26 FRELIMO (Frente de Libertação de Moçambique) is a democratic socialist political party in Mozambique. It is the dominant party in Mozambique and has won a majority of the seats in the Assembly of the Republic in every election since the country's first multi-party election in 1994.

revolutionary internationalists, and that's what the Black Panther Party was about ideologically. And you have to know that to understand where it's going. Came from a Black liberation struggle into understanding that our liberation was absolutely and inextricably tied to the liberation of all people, of oppressed people of the world. And when we see that we will begin to understand what struggle is about.

[Applause]

I want to say briefly that we had an agenda. We had an ideology. We were communist with a small 'c'. We could've been any number of other things, but for the sake of argument right now we'll just say we were communists with a small 'c'. Certainly not communists with a big 'C'. We were not being operated by those reactionaries in Moscow. We had an agenda. Our agenda was our platform and program as I've mentioned. We had strategy. Our strategy had to do with survival programs – what we called our survival programs – under the slogan: "survival pending revolution." That is to say, how can you talk about organizing people when they can't get healthcare? It's very difficult getting up in the morning, talking about revolution now when you have breast cancer. It's very difficult to get up when your children are dying of toxic mold in the walls, so we started talking about health clinics, free clinics for the people, free food for the people, free busing to prisons program cause so many people were in prison.

And of course, we were identified as the greatest threat to the internal security of the United States by the FBI and other agencies of the government who raised up COINTELPRO[27] and put it down on us as hard as it came down on anybody at all. With the murder of Fred Hampton[28] and other people murdered in our organization and so forth and so on.

At the same time we struggled very hard to try to change the minds and hearts of people in this country so that we could begin to build a revolutionary force. Now, we can talk about some of the mistakes we made and I hope that

---

27 COINTELPRO (Counter Intelligence Program, 1956-1971) was a series of covert and illegal projects actively conducted by the FBI aimed at surveilling, infiltrating, discrediting, and disrupting domestic American political organizations.

28 Fred Hampton Sr. (1948-1969) came to prominence in Chicago as deputy chairman of the national Black Panther Party. In 1967, the FBI identified Hampton as a radical threat. In December 1969, Hampton was drugged, shot and killed in his bed during a predawn raid at his Chicago apartment by a tactical unit of the Cook County State's Attorney's Office. In 1990, Chicago City Council declared a Fred Hampton Day of commemoration in Chicago.

you'll ask me those questions. Our ideal that we were gonna have revolution now, that just because we thought about it and clicked our heels together three times, revolutionary change was going to occur, that we didn't have to do any real work – and we did do real work. We did our survival program. We did all of that. But we were crushed from within and from without.

I think the one thing I wanna leave you with right now in this time that I have remaining is to talk about the conditions today, because for Black people the conditions are effectively the same as they were in 1966 when the Black Panther Party was started. As a matter of fact it might be worse.

We have massive poverty in America, not only among Blacks but among whites. We have the resegregation as I said of American schools and of affirmative action. Black infant mortality is the same as it was then: double that of white infant mortality. So-called Black wealth, Blacks own one percent of all business revenues in the United States of America from Blacks. And then we have the thing I want to focus our attention on, as far as my talk is concerned, is the new slavery.

We have two million people in the United States who are in prisons and over six million people who have been in prison or are in prison collectively today in the United States of America. Of course, we have the largest incarceration and maintain the largest prison system in the world. This is the United States of America. I know that you know that, I know you know about the three-strikes crime bills, I know you know that people are going to prison for drugs, but I know one of the things that you have to realize is that we're not only incarcerating ... fifty percent of those people who are incarcerated are Black. Over one million people in prison who are Black. The question is why is this true and how did it come to be true? This all goes to a new age of racism in America where we pretend we don't really have racism because it all died somehow with Martin Luther King and everything was okay and we don't know what's wrong today. And we have children who are in prison, particularly young Black boys throughout America – millions of them.

So what I'm hoping today is that we get to talk about where we can go, that the most important thing that we have to discuss among ourselves, of all these tendencies that you have and all these interests that you have – whether you're talking about women's issues or gay issues or human rights or animal rights or environmental questions or world trade organizations or any other things that you're talking about – that we have to have a common ideology, and we have to have some common goals, and we have to stop being so arrogant that we think we're the ones with the answers, because you see, the masses of people are not here. Masses of people here in DC are Black, and they're not here. [Applause] So one of the things we have to know is how we're gonna move beyond this moment right here and organize ourselves toward a true agenda of liberation and freedom, and I hope that that's where we're going, because revolutionary change must take place, we're in a stage – we've finally reached the ultimate stage and that's global fascism. And it's not just been led by Bush. Clinton put a lot of pieces in play.

And so, I want to close by saying that in our questions and in our answers and in our discussion, the one thing that I hope that you will take away today is what can we do together that's really going to galvanize the masses of people in this country because we have the duty as Americans, because this country is in charge of the world – it has all the guns, it has all the money – everybody else is a subject of this country. There are hardly any more countries to speak of – from France to China, they all don't matter because there's only one army, and that army is led by George Bush[29] and Dick Cheney[30] and Halliburton[31] and whatever else there is, and we don't even know what some of these pieces are. It's time for us to take this down and it's time for us to form a serious agenda. It's not enough to have a ring in your nose and wear some dreadlocks or whatever else you're doing with your cultural style questions. The bottom line is we have to reach the masses of people and create the kind of struggle where we can really truly bring about a new wave of energy so we can talk about revolutionary worldwide revolution and have an enlightened and new society where truly there is a redistribution of wealth, and human beings have all things we need to live a decent life.

[Applause]

---

29 George W. Bush (born 1946) was governor of Texas between 1995 and 2000, and President of the United States between 2001 and 2009. (His father, George H.W. Bush, was President from 1989 to 1993.)
30 Dick Cheney (born 1941) served as the vice president of the United States from 2001 to 2009 under President George W. Bush.
31 Halliburton is an American multinational corporation responsible for most of the world's hydraulic fracturing operations. The company has been criticized for its involvement in numerous controversies, including its involvement with Dick Cheney and the Iraq War.

Ericka Huggins and Talibah Shakir

Ericka Huggins joined the Black Panther Party for Self Defense (BPP) in 1968 along with her husband John Jerome Huggins. In 1969 she moved to New Haven, Connecticut where she spent two years in prison, accused of the murder of Alex Rackley. She was acquitted in 1971 and returned to California, becoming director of the Oakland Community School from 1973-1981. This program, entitled "Servants of the People Still," aired February 5, 2004.

Today we are going to be hearing the voices of two very wonderful and beautiful comrade sisters – members of the Black Panther Party for Self Defense – here in Los Angeles, California. January 17 was the 35th anniversary of the assassination of Bunchy Carter and John Huggins[1] on the campus of UCLA. John Huggins was married to Ericka Huggins, and they had a three-week-old baby at the time. Alprentice Bunchy Carter was the de facto leader of the southern California chanpter of the Black Panther Party at that time and his leadership style was one of creating leaders wherever he went. They were murdered on January 17, 1969, on the campus of UCLA.

I wanted to do this show in January, but, as we have all heard and experienced and said, things happen for a reason. We're bringing you the show today.

---

1 John Jerome Huggins Jr. (1945-1969) was the leader in the Los Angeles chapter of the Black Panther Party who was killed on the UCLA campus in January 1969.

Let me state however, that before we get into these interviews that I have conducted with Ericka Huggins and Talibah Shakir, a member of the Los Angeles Black Panther Party at that time, let me go into my brief commentary.

Today's show, as I said, is about these two comrade sisters: Ericka Huggins, Talibah Shakir, and their experiences being in the Black Panther Party in Los Angeles in the 1960s. That was a time of great upheaval, of great social change and unrest. The Black Panther Party came on the scene and it captured the imagination of a generation of people – not just Black people, but young whites, Puerto Ricans, Mexicanos, Asian-Americans – all those people who were about change and social justice and revolution in this country. The Black Panther Party lit a fire under the United States of America, which is why J. Edgar Hoover had to extinguish it – had to smash it. I wanted to talk to these sisters about their experiences.

We're going to talk first with Ericka Huggins. I had an opportunity to sit down with her last Saturday in Oakland, California. She was eating lunch, and you're going to hear the noises in the background of the people around us in the cafeteria eating lunch, and I had no choice – I couldn't move. I was mesmerized by this sister's story. So we're going to go to some clips of that and come back, and talk more about Ericka, and talk to Talibah, and some other things. For now, let's meet Ericka Huggins.

Ericka Huggins: People often want to interview me, or Angela Davis[2] or Elaine Brown or Kathleen Cleaver[3] because they figure: "oh, they are brave." I want to say that I have the powerful belief that you are brave, and that I think that everybody you know and I know are brave, and that if they are women, they are brave women. They're just living life with as much integrity as possible. With as much kindness as possible. With as much mindfulness as possible.

Thandisizwe Chimurenga: And you have always felt that way?

---

2 Angela Davis (born 1944) is an American scholar, activist, and author who is known for her work in social justice movements, particularly in the areas of race, gender, and prison abolition. She became a professor of philosophy at the University of California but was dismissed in 1970 due to her political activism and affiliation with the Communist Party USA. Throughout her career, Davis has been an outspoken advocate for the rights of oppressed and marginalized communities.

3 Kathleen Neal Cleaver (born 1945) is an American law professor and activist, known for her involvement with the Black Power movement and the Black Panther Party. She married Eldridge Cleaver in 1967 and stayed married to him for for 20 years,

EH: I have always felt that way. Always. And because of that, my mother and my father considered me a supreme idealist. I have always felt that way, that's why when I met John Huggins, and then a few months later read about Huey Newton being shot by a police officer and charged with the killing of another police officer, that I wanted to leave Lincoln University where I was sitting, and go and join his defense committee and support the upliftment of people.

While I was there, by the way, was a very powerful time at Lincoln. The year that I left, Charles Hamilton[4] was in residence there, and he and Stokely Carmichael[5] were writing the book *Black Power*. There was so much going on within me and in society hat led me to be pretty fierce about living a life about freedom. This is why I joined the Black Panther Party: At the time I thought that freedom was something, as I mentioned to you before, that would occur if there were economic or social or class or racial obstacles moved out of the way. And that's true also, but if a person who's striving toward freedom hasn't done the work inside themselves to break those chains, the external forces mean nothing.

Think about it. Think about all the people you may have heard about, if you don't know them personally, who have all the resources in place – have friends, family, everything – and they're lonely or bitter or at the least unhappy people. There is something more in life that I always wanted to know about. And that something more that I wanted to know about led me to work on behalf of poor and Black people – not that I grew up rich, but that was the frame I held people in.

I grew up in Washington, DC actually, and what I saw was capital hill, and where I lived in southeast DC – two different worlds. A lot of things compelled me to join the party, and one of them was that I don't like to see anybody suffer – no living being. And yes, I've always felt that way. And since I'm born in an African-American body and in a woman's body, I'm naturally wired to think that way with a compassionate view. I think those

---

4 Charles Hamilton (1929-) is a political scientist, civil rights leader, and a professor emeritus at Columbia University. His most noted work is *Black Power: The Politics of Liberation*, written with Stokely Carmichael.
5 Stokely Carmichael, also known as Kwame Ture (1941-1996), was a civil rights activist and leader in the U.S. during the 1960s. He was born in Trinidad and immigrated to the U.S. with his family as a child. He became the chairman of the Student Nonviolent Coordinating Committee (SNCC) in 1966. He changed his name to Kwame Ture in 1978 to honor two African leaders, Kwame Nkrumah of Ghana and Ahmed Sékou Touré of Guinea.

two things can lead you to a compassionate view if you allow them, rather than a retaliatory view, which is easy to have as women and as women of color. I just don't choose to be retaliatory because it makes me sick. I don't know what it does to anybody else, but it makes me sick.

And that was something that I came to when I was in Niantic Prison. But let me back up for a little bit, because we haven't gotten to prison yet.

I met John Huggins on the Lincoln University campus and decided that it was time for me to go. The police were outright shooting people for no good reason. I wanted to be a part of the end to that in whatever way that I could, so I asked him if we could use his car to drive across the country. By then we were just friends and later we fell in love. When we got to Los Angeles, which was around Thanksgiving time of 1967, we got married, and eventually he became a part of the High Potential program at UCLA. High Potential was a precursor of affirmative action programs, making a way for African-American and Latino students to become students – to apply and receive financial aid and really matriculate the campus. And programs like that were blossoming around the country.

We have forgotten – and I say "we" American people have forgotten – the reason why we even had Affirmative Action[6] in the first place. That the sons and daughters of colonized Mexico and the sons and daughters and great grand children of enslaved Americans from Africa – the fact that they could think about going to college was more a part of current history, and that they'd be given a fair chance in applying to, for instance, a UC campus, was pretty miraculous. The High Potential program afforded a number of wonderful young people to seek additional education.

So John Huggins and Bunchy Carter were part of that group, and as such, the Black Student Unions were cropping up all over the country. That concept, actually, was started by the Black Panther Party. I don't really care if men started it or women started it. It was started by the Black Panther Party, which didn't really have time on a day-to-day basis to think about how important it was to be a woman or how important it was to be a man,

---

6 Affirmative Action in the U.S. refers to policies and practices that aim to provide equal opportunities and redress historical and ongoing discrimination against certain marginalized groups, primarily based on race, gender, and ethnicity. Affirmative Action traces its roots back to the civil rights movement of the 1960s but has been a topic of intense debate and has faced legal challenges throughout its history.

but we were aware that there were ways that we had been conditioned by society to believe that men were more powerful and women less so. Except that the FBI and the police all over this country were killing the men in the party rapidly and allowing the women to live. So from a political and social standpoint we started to explore that and study that as a group, and we realized that women were not seen as an equal danger. It's kind of ironic, isn't it?

Because so many men in the party were being killed or jailed, the women actually ran the party after a point. This was not something that the leadership of the party thought – this was something that was accepted by most of the men. Cause most of the men in the party at the leadership level were open and clear and honest about their places of backwardness or their progressive understanding. Huey Newton, by the way, was a feminist man. John Huggins was a feminist man, and so was Alprentice Carter.

One thing I will say about Alprentice Carter is that at the same time, he held what I would consider to be a residual African awareness of women as those who we protect in our society because they give birth to children. It wasn't demeaning at all. He was very loving and caring of all of us. I remember that this man was so busy continually and in such a hot seat, could remember that it was my 20th birthday.

I hope your listeners are looking at what keeps them from fully loving others, whatever package they're born into – particularly women of color. One of the things that I notice about our illnesses and our sufferings and our sicknesses as they express themselves, because we suffer from Post-Traumatic Slave Syndrome, and that is not a term of my own. That is a term that I learned from Dr Joy DeGruy[7] and if you ever have an opportunity to hear her speak or to hear her CDs – you can connect with her talks through The Power of Oneness organization. She's incredible, and this is what she talks about.

It's phenomenal to me how well we know how to hate. How well we know how to understand separation, and how little we know about active loving of one another. I'm not talking about the people that are just the closest to us. Perhaps we know how to do that. We want to know that

---

7 Dr. Joy Angela DeGruy (1957-) is an author, academic, and researcher. She is best known for her book *Post Traumatic Slave Syndrome*, originally published in 2005 and republished in 2017.

without creating more separation. I'm saying that now to women of color, and I'm saying that specifically to African-American women who might be listening.

TC: Ericka Huggins, after the assassination of her husband, accompanied his body back to New Haven, Connecticut. In this next segment she talks about her experience there. The Counter Intelligence Program of the FBI framed Ericka Huggins on a murder charge, and she spent almost two years in Niantic Prison. During this time, she says she utilized it to get to know herself better in the places and areas where she needed work so that she could continue to work for the people – the same work that she did in the Black Panther Party.

EH: After Alprentice Carter and John Huggins were killed, it was a tipping point in my life – as I told you I was barely 20 years old and I was the mother of a three-week-old. They were killed not just because the Us Organization was nationalist and we were more in the socialist vein, not just because the students didn't want Ronald Everett – Ron Karenga[8] – to be the High Potential program director. They wanted someone else from the community to be the High Potential program director. Not because of those surface things, but because the government of the United States at the time did not want the Black Panther Party to exist. In 1969, John Mitchell,[9] who was then the Attorney General, said: "we will wipe out the Black Panther Party by the end of 1969 by any means necessary."

What happened on the UCLA campus was directly related. The FBI's Counter Intelligence Program placed a number of organizations and individuals under surveillance, and the Black Panther Party was definitely under surveillance – all of its leading members, which would include John Huggins, Bunchy Carter and many, many others, and of course, eventually myself.

They were killed and I went to New Haven to bury John's body, and Bunchy's family buried him near, and I thought that I would be coming back to California shortly thereafter, but the Black [inaudible] in New Haven,

---

8 Ron Karenga, also known as Maulana Karenga (1941-), is an American activist, author, and professor of Africana studies. At the time, he was leader of a group called the Us Organization.
9 John Mitchell (1913-1988) was the 67th Attorney General of the United States under President Richard Nixon. He was tried and convicted as a result of his involvement in the Watergate scandal.

Connecticut – John had grown up in New Haven, Connecticut. That's why I had gone to the East Coast. The students asked me to stay to start a chapter of the party there, and I did stay. Then three months later, I was arrested for conspiracy with the intent to commite murder. A man was murdered. I did not murder him. Again, I felt that this was a part of the FBI's Counter Intelligence Program.

I was arrested and I was held awaiting trial for 14 months. After that time, the trial took six months, three months of which was just to pick the jury because the climate was so vile. The charges against me were dropped and I was released, but in that two year period of time that I was inside the external prison, I got to look at a way in which my heart had been chained over time, and the ways in which I knew I needed to improve my relationship to myself and to others. I spent a lot of time alone because due to our political beliefs we were not allowed to be – when I was arrested there were six women arrested. We were not allowed to be in the general inmate population. We were sequestered, the six of us, and over the first year that I was incarcerated, gradually they let the other women go. They were interested in meeting members of the party and wiping out members of the Black Panther Party as John Mitchell said. Pretty soon I was in solitary confinement.

I used that time to teach myself about myself and to look at my own reflection. I could see where because my father had been an alcoholic and was very unkind to my mother, how I had embibed some of her condition and some of his. I could see the way in which I wanted to raise my child if I ever would be released. I wasn't sure that I would be. I could see that I needed to have an internal contentment in order to meet life from day to day that I didn't have, so I taught myself to meditate. I also set up for myself a program of exercise, which included [inaudible] yoga. No one told me to do this. This is something that I felt motivated to do because I knew that if your mind is [inaudible], you can be in touch with your heart. Once you're in touch with your heart – and I'm not talking about your hear that beats, I'm talking about your inner being – than everything is confluent from there. I knew this. I can't describe how I knew it, but any of the brave people I've ever read about in life have all said the same thing. So that's what I did to keep myself sane and aware while I was there, and to keep myself from missing my daughter so much. She was a baby of three months, and she was two-and-a-half when I was released. Being able to see her for an hour on each Saturday for months and months wasn't fun.

I was released a different person than the person who went in. That stayed with me – this feeling of the deeper freedom that we can attain stayed with me. There were many, many times when I was incarcerated that I knew that even if I had the keys to walk out, would that make me free? No. If I had money, would that make me free? No. Having some keys and having some money would be helpful, but it wouldn't give me the freedom that we're talking about when we're talking about freedom. What I found out is that no one can give it to me. It is already there, if I know how to access it. There were many times that I felt absolutely free in prison because I allowed no one to hold me in bondage. This was quite a mystery to the prison authorities, because I would ask them to do things like lock me in rather than watch television. "Please don't give me any bread and potatoes because it makes me sluggish and I want to be aware while I'm here." They couldn't hate me because they couldn't figure out what to hate me for, and I wasn't trusted. I'm glad I wasn't trusted by them. I met many, many women who were prison guards who were like angels. All the prison guards in New Haven, Connecticut, between 1969 and '71 were white. I can't think of one guard of color from any background. Most of the women were African-American, Puerto Rican, Dominican and from the islands, and there were poor white women. But the guards were white.

But I met two angels, one of whom came to me one day and gave me her keys and said: "You know, you really don't belong here. Why don't you just go? I'll take the weight for it."

TC: She actually said that?

EH: She put the keys in my hand. I can still see her. I have no idea where she is, nor do I remember what her last name anymore, but I remember her face and I remember her heart. It was such purity, and there was no dirty motivation behind her. She wasn't trying to set me up. But I told her no. That if I walked, my daughter would never know the truth that I wanted her to know: that I didn't kill anybody. The people who were depending on me and supporting my child would never know: is this a fabricated charge or is it not? So I wanted to do what was my duty, and so I stayed, but I've never forgotten that woman. As a matter of fact, that was a very uplifting moment in my life, and it gave me a renewed hope in humanity.

[Plays Gil Scott-Heron[10]'s Whitey On The Moon]

TC: The Black Panther Party for Self Defense was an anti-racist organization. One of their principles when they first started said they wanted an end to the robberies of their communities by the white man. They subsequently evolved their thinking and said they wanted an end to the robbery of their community by the racist capitalists. Gil Scott-Heron's work *Whitey on the Moon* was written in 1970. It was Neil Armstrong who first walked on the moon for the United States in 1969, so this was the climate that was back then, but it is still relevant today.

Let me say that if there were any of our KPFK listeners who were offended by our use of "Whitey" we apologize, but just substitute, when you hear *Whitey on the Moon* just substitute *W on the Rover*. It still applies: "A rat done bit my sister Nell and W's on the rover. I can't pay no doctor bills but W's on the rover." Where have I heard that before? Not having any healthcare? Something was happening recently, maybe locally, about not having healthcare. Anyway, it applies today – the words that Gil Scott-Heron spoke, just like the work of the Black Panther Party still applies today.

As I said, we also talked to Talibah Shakir. Talibah Shakir is a teacher in the Los Angeles Unified School District, and I asked her to tell us about her experiences as a teenager in the Black Panther Party here in Los Angeles.

Talibah Shakir: Around 1968 I joined the Black Panther Party on 84th and Broadway. I was introduced to the Black Panther Party by Roland Freeman. Later after that I met Bunchy Carter. I had heard about Bunchy some years before because he was a former Slauson and my brother was a Gladiator,[11] so they used to war – like what we seein' today between the Bloods and the Crips.

TC: Those were the names of the gangs at that time.

---

10 Gil Scott-Heron (1949-2011) was an American poet, musician, and author known for his influence on spoken word poetry, jazz, and soul music. Scott-Heron's works often addressed social and political issues, including racism, poverty, and the struggles faced by African-Americans. He is best known for "The Revolution Will Not Be Televised," released in 1970.

11 Gangs that preceded Crips and Bloods.

TS: Yeah, but it was a lot different – fist fights and go home. Not all the murder, not the drive-by's, just a fist fight and go home.

TC: So you heard about Bunchy Carter?

TS: Yeah, he was a legend in his own time. I was hanging out at a pool hall – All Nation Pool Hall – on 84th and Broadway. You have to understand, I came up in a strict household with Southern values and my mother had three daughters, and we were all close in age. Real strict, you know? She messed around and got a job at the telephone company, swing shift. When she went to work, I was out swingin'. I would leave and go down to Broadway and 84th to the All Nation Pool Hall, and one day I saw Roland standing in the doorway. He said, "come here, come here." And I said, "no, I'm not coming, I'm not coming." He said, "do you know who you are?" I said "I know who I am." He said, "you must not," because at that time I was into drinkin', droppin' red devils, doin' anything else a teenager would do in this day, you know?

TC: How old were you at this point?

TS: I was 16, right before my 17th birthday.

TC: And Roland was asking who you were. What did he mean by that?

TS: What he meant was historically, did I know who I was. That I was descended from kings and queens, and we had a struggle before us, and we had to regain our tradition of greatness. That's what he was trying to get from me. He was trying to evoke that answer from me. It was not my name or where you live or whatever. Do you know who you are historically and what your place should be in this world? I guess he saw something inside of me that I didn't know I had.

TC: From that initial meeting with Roland you were subsequently, other meetings or what have you, going to events?

TS: Actually, I was kind of mad at him for even putting me on the spot like that because I had two of my little partners with me, so I went across the street to the pool hall. I was trying to dance, you know, get my groove on. I used to dance then. But I just couldn't cut a step because every time I got up to dance I could just hear his words resounding: "do you know who you are? Do you know who you are?"

So I snuck outside the pool hall, went back across the street to the Black

Panther office, and they was havin' a political education class. I had no idea what that was, but he invited me in to read. He knew I was drunk and I felt he was trying to make fun of me. So I was readin' a Black Panther newspaper. He asked me to read a passage and he asked me if I could interpret it.

Well, I could read. That was one thing my mother made sure – all her children could read and comprehend what they read, so I broke it down. And I felt like I had got back at him cause everybody was just shocked and amazed that, here this little girl had come, she's drunk, hangin' out, and she's runnin' it like that. So I was glad that I had got back at him, and I just left to go back across the street to the pool hall. Even later in the night his words just kept coming back.

I was a student at Fremont High School, and I went to school the next day. I kept hearing these words and I was like, "I wish he would just get out of my head." I was just fightin' and I didn't want to hear about it. Two days later, my school was on 76th and San Pedro, and I lived on 88th place and San Pedro, so I didn't have any reason to go around the Black Panther office. I just found myself every day going the long way home, hanging out around around the office, seeing what I could do, learnin' stuff.

Within a week or two I understood the question was "do you know who you are?" and I knew what I needed to do to help our people regain their traditional greatness.

TC: Now let's fast forward to December of 1968, the shootout on Central Avenue. Your office was on…

TS: 84th and Broadway, and the shootout was at our headquarters which is 41st and Central.

TC: So you had a Panther headquarters, and for lack of a better word, affiliate offices throughout LA?

TS: Yes.

TC: What did that look like in terms of the Black Panther Party presence in Los Angeles, in terms of members, in terms of where you guys were located, where the work was. Paint a picture for us.

TS: We were strategically located in the Black community where the most police abuse happened. We had an office on 84th and Broadway, we had one out in Compton later, we had one out on 55th and Broadway. So we were all over the city. Sometimes just some little houses. If we were not in an office, we had different cells where people would go out into the community and interact with different people. We were basically the vanguard for the people.

TC: I'm going to get to December of '68 in a moment. From the time that you joined, give us an example of what your daily tasks would be. What would you do when you would get to the Panther office? You were in high school at the time, right?

TS: I was in high school.

TC: So you would leave school... when you went to school. When you went to school you would leave school and go to the Panther office, or maybe you would go the Panther office early. What would you do?

TS: I'ma have to be honest. I was at school, and I would go there after school. Then, all of a sudden, I started going there at lunch time. 1st, 2nd, 3rd, 4th, 5th period I was there. Every other day I was there at the Panther office.

First of all, when I joined the Black Panther Party it was different from when people joined in the 1970s. When I joined, you had to go through a probationary period to show that you were really involved and committed to the struggle. I had to learn the ten-point platform. I had to go interact with community members. They observed me if something happened in the community – some type of police action, what would my reaction be? Basically they had to know: Was you scared or were you going to stand up? And I had to learn all that. We learned different forms of medical treatments, we learned how to use various types of guns for self defense only, we learned how to break them down, clean them. We had learned a lot of things because that was a matter of survival, but we also must ad that we were always taught: Do not start anything, but you have the right to self defense by any means necessary.

TC: So you would find yourself sometimes leaving school early and sometimes not going to school. Now, you're 16, going on 17 years of age. You're a teenager, a young girl. Was there ever a time that you felt unsafe because you were a young woman?

TS: Never, because the brothers in the Party became brothers to me. When the community residents knew we were on the street, we were loved by everybody. That was a time when in America, Blacks referred to each other as "my sister", "my brother". It was truly Black love everywhere we went. And the Black Panthers, we had a lot of respect. If we went to the market, if we went to the barber shop, people respected us. At that time you could walk all over town and nobody bothered you. I didn't feel threatened because I knew what we had to do.

I knew there was a possibility of death happening, but when you focused and there's something you believe in, that's the least of your concern.

TC: I understand what you're saying in terms of outside of the Black Panther Party, but from older men inside the Black Panther Party, at no time did you feel that your safety was in jeopardy?

TS: Not at all. The Black Panther Party, you have to understand, there was a lot of youngsters there. I was probably one of the youngest sisters in the Black Panther Party. Most of the people were in their twenties, in college, what have you. Looking back I know a lot of our parents were upset with us because we joined the Black Panther Party, but it was no orgies goin' on, it was nothing like that. No temptation. Because our model was revolution first, not you and I as individuals. The older brothers took me under their wing. I became their sister and they protected me and they loved me as if I was from their mother. There was never any threat. Never.

TC: You would go out into the community, and, as you said, they wanted to see how you would perform under pressure and how you would react. What about political education? Were there tasks that you had to carry out in the community? Working for the newspaper? Making flyers? How did you go about politicizing other members and community members?

TS: We had – I think it was called a Duplo machine or something like that. We used to type it up and roll it out to make our little newsletters. Basically what we'd do was we'd come out and talk to community members about the politics affecting their community. About the oppression in the community. Also, resources in the community. We had that type of information for the people, and if the people had a problem – say it was an altercation with the police that was unjust, I saw that. I had to stop and assess the situation – get the officer's name and number, find out who the person was, and 99 percent of the time we would bail the person if they were bailable, and we would get them an attorney, so we had to do that. That was a part of our political training within the Black Panther Party.

TC: We come to December of 1968. Black Panther Party in Los Angeles had affiliate offices. Yours was on 84th and Broadway. The headquarters at that time was on 41st and Central Avenue. It became what was known as the Panthers Shootout, or the Shoot-In. Tell us about that.

TS: There was 13 Panthers in the office, and what they were charged with was conspiracy to murder a police officer. I always thought that was ironic because if you were gonna murder somebody, you would go to where they are. They wouldn't come to you. And this is basically what happened with the Panthers.

They were inside the building and the police came, and as we used to say, bamped on the Panther members. It was like all out war that day. They was actually shootin' with all types of military weapons. This was LA, with a group of young Black people. And they were shootin' them as if they were in a war with another country.

TC: There was a standoff of several hours. Eventually the Panthers came out, and they were charged with attempted murder on police officers.

TS: Conspiracy to murder police officers among a whole host of other charges.

TC: What eventually came of those charges?

TS: They went to trial. They were known as the LA 13. They went to the courthouse, the Hall of Justice – a jail that used to be at 1st and Broadway across the street from the new criminal courts building. They went to trial in 1970 or '71 I believe, and they went through court. After 13 people that were involved in the shootout, Paul Redd who later became my husband, he was sentenced to six years in Soledad State Prison. I believe another guy by the name of Will did a few months, but Paul Redd did the most time in Soledad. The charges were dropped against the other members, and during that time a lot of us were contacted by the police, myself included. Police of the FBI asked us to tell on Geronimo Pratt,[12] something about

---

12 Elmer "Geronimo" Pratt (1947-2011) was a decorated military veteran and a high-ranking member of the Black Panther Party in the late 1960s and early 1970s. The FBI targeted Pratt in a COINTELPRO operation. He served 27 years in prison and was freed in 1997 when his conviction was quashed due to the prosecution's having

Geronimo Pratt, so that my husband could be set free. My response was, "We're in it to win for our people and whatever happened, happened."

TC: January 1969, members of the Black Panther Party are also students at UCLA along with members of the Us Organization.[13] Why don't you tell us about that time period after the shoot-in at the Panther headquarters.

TS: What I had understood had happened was there was some type of squabble or confrontation about some type of Black studies program that was going to be implemented at UCLA. Ron Karenga wanted to be head of the program and so did some of the Black Panther members. I don't know exactly what happened because I was not there, but later on in the evening I heard about the shootout. Alprentice Bunchy Carter and John Huggins were shot by members of the Us Organization.

TC: What had been happening on the campus at UCLA? The Panthers were in the community. You were in Compton, you were at 55th and Broadway, but you were also at UCLA. What was the work that was going on at that time?

TS: At UCLA they had some type of program. Any time an activist applied to UCLA, we got in on full scholarship. They had even gave me one, and I hadn't even finished high school and I just didn't go, because I was out here working for the people. Later I had found out that it was some type of program by the government to let all these activists in to keep watch over. But I wasn't really clear on it because I didn't go to UCLA. I was in the community and I very seldom had to go up there at all, but there was this program and the Panthers wanted to be in this position on this program.

TC: Bunchy Carter and John Huggins are murdered at UCLA. You had an opportunity to go to that meeting, but you didn't get a ride from Bunchy. Let's go back: You just found out about what was happening. What do you do next? What goes on?

TS: I was in shock. I was in complete shock. It hurt because first of all I kept

---

withheld evidence that proved his innocence. Pratt was the godfather of the late rapper Tupac Shakur.
13 Us Organization is a Black nationalist group in the United States founded in 1965. It was established as a community organization by Hakim Jamal together with Maulana Karenga. The Black Panthers and Us had different aims and tactics but often found themselves competing for potential recruits. The FBI intensified this antipathy as part of its COINTELPRO operations. On January 17, 1969, a gun battle between the groups on the UCLA campus ended in the deaths of John Huggins and Alprentice "Bunchy" Carter. Later in 1969, two other Black Panther members were killed and one other was wounded by Us members.

thinking, had I been there, would the outcome had been different? Maybe we might not be in there, was I responsible? It really hurt me. Bunchy Carter was a beautiful brother in spirit, and the way he trained us just gave us pride. John Huggins, his wife Ericka was pregnant. And we used to talk all the time, and I thought about her. I cried for her, I cried for her baby. It was just horrible. But the news had reported that two students were killed, and I called because I believe John and Bunchy deserved their props, and I told 'em they were not only students there but they were ranking members of the Black Panther Party.

TC: So you called the news to tell them?

TS: Yes I did, yes I did. Later, some Panther friends of mine, we went and met at this house on 84th and Flower, and first of all we poured out a drink, pouring libation for Bunchy and John. Basically what that was, was dark port wine and lemon juice. That was the drink of the Panthers, and we poured it out in libation and we sat and we talked about when we met Bunchy and John and the impact they had on our lives. It was a lot of tears and a lot of pain that night. A lot.

TC: From that night, what was your next move as an organization here in Los Angeles?

TS: First of all, we did our own investigation We wanted to find out what happened to Bunchy and John at UCLA. We wanted to find out who was involved. Most people would have thought our next move would be to retaliate against the Us Organization, but it wasn't. We was organized because what we believed led up to this was, we had been getting letters and notes supposedly from the Us Organization, and we had already understood that was part of the government's program COINTELPRO[14] to keep us warring at each other and maybe killin' each other off. So we used to try to meet with the Us Organization and tell them we weren't trying to do this. We knew this was coming from the government or some outside person, just trying to aggravate us, and we were not going for it. We knew as tragic as it was with the death of Bunchy and John that this was another plan to somehow destroy the Black Panther Party.

---

14 COINTELPRO (Counter Intelligence Program, 1956-1971) was a series of covert and illegal projects actively conducted by the FBI aimed at surveilling, infiltrating, discrediting, and disrupting domestic American political organizations.

TC: So you conducted your own investigation, or you began the steps to conduct your own investigation. And the funeral for John and Bunchy...

TS: John Huggins didn't have his funeral here in Los Angeles. His body was flown home. I think he came from Connecticut. Bunchy Carter had his funeral here at Trinity Baptist Church, and I served as one of the ushers there. I was at the front door letting people come in, and I remember Sammy Davis Jr[15] came, Nancy Wilson[16] came, it was like a funeral for the heads of state. The most beautiful thing I remembered about that funeral was that it seemed like all of California cried for Bunchy because it rained that day, and that time of year it was unusual for rain. It rained, and the caravan was so long, we didn't have enough motorcycle escorts until Panther members got outside and stopped traffic. We had cars just coming in. They got out with their shotguns and doing it Panther style. We stopped traffic. Nobody was cuttin' in on this.

Bunchy had a yellow '65 Mustang, and somebody had the Mustang in the funeral procession. It was long. It was as far as the eye could see and beyond. It was long. And the brothers got out and the rain was pouring. It was just like the whole world was cryin' for Bunchy, and we buried him out on Central Avenue, I think close to Artesia. We gave Bunchy a token. I threw earrings into the casket. Other people started pouring things into the casket.

One thing I was proud of was that Bunchy was buried with my red book – the little book that we studied by Mao Tse-Tung.[17] He was buried with my red book in his hands.

TC: I'm just thinkin' 'bout that, must've been a heck of a funeral, and a heck of a funeral procession.

TS: It was. And the police stayed back. They stayed way back. Cause it was to the point like – I think if something would've happened I might not be

---

15 Sammy Davis Jr. (1925-1990) was a Black American entertainer known for his work as a singer, dancer, and actor. Despite his success, Davis faced racism and discrimination throughout his life. He refused to perform at segregated venues and was a member of the NAACP and other civil rights organizations.

16 Nancy Wilson (1937-2018) was an American singer whose career spanned over five decades. Wilson recorded more than 70 albums and won three Grammy Awards for her work. She also had her own series on NBC, The Nancy Wilson Show (1967–1968), which won an Emmy. In September 2005, Wilson was inducted into the International Civil Rights Walk of Fame at the Martin Luther King Jr. National Historic Site.

17 Mao Zedong (1893-1976), also transcribed as Mao Tse-Tung, was a Chinese communist revolutionary who was the founder of the People's Republic of China (PRC) which he led from 1949 until his death in 1976. The *Little Red Book* is a book of statements from speeches and writing, first published in 1964. The book's popularity and influence spread beyond China and it became a revolutionary icon around the world.

here today, because that's how deep it was. You see brothers gettin' out in the rain, shotguns in the intersections in LA, and nobody's touchin' 'em. It was deep. It was deep.

And even talking about it now, it still hurts. That was unnecessary death. All the deaths that occurred in the '60s for our liberation was unnecessary, because what people have to understand – if that condition did not exist in America we would not start organizations like the Black Panther Party, SNCC, CORE, NAACP – none of that would've happened if it was not for the conditions that created the need to have these organizations.

TC: My name is Thandisizwe Chimurenga, and today we're talking to Talibah Shakir and Ericka Huggins regarding their experiences in the Black Panther Party here in Los Angeles 35 years after the murders of Alprentice Bunchy Carter and John Huggins on the campus of UCLA. Ericka Huggins and Talibah Shakir, as you have heard today, have some differing recollections of certain incidents that went on at that time. They have also taken different paths since 1969, however they both have remained active and committed to people – the liberation of people from bondage. Ericka Huggins is a leading member of a Siddha Yoga community in Northern California. In asking her what Siddha Yoga was, she told me: "it's a yoga that believes that all human beings hold within them a great power that once awakened can move through a human being and transform any limited understanding they may have of themselves, their world or others, and leads to the state of contentment and tranquility that I longed for when I was in prison." I was asking Ericka to tell me about what she was doing now. I asked her where she was now:

EH: That's a great question. I am where I always wanted to be: with people who are willing to be brave about their dark places inside, so that the light of their awareness can shine outward. I'm happy to say that I work with young people, which is something that I did before I joined the Black Panther Party. During the time that I was in the Black Panther Party, I ran the Oakland Community School for ten years. I also taught meditation to those children that came through that school. The school was predominantly African-American and Latino in East Oakland. So I've continued to work with young people, and now my responsibility is to work with them around the globe, wherever they are around the globe – young people who are interested in the great power that exists inside. Since we're always looking for power, working with young people I know they're quite aware of that power. And it's easily accessible because it's right there inside.

TC: Like Ericka Huggins, Talibah Shakir also spent time in jail. Her "crime" was ostensibly the same as Ericka's – i.e. being a member of the Black Panther Party – but it was not the state that put her in jail, it was her own family. When I asked Talibah about where she was today and what she was doing, Talibah told me she was a teacher. Actually, Talibah is what we call a community educator. She's been one since her days in the Black Panther Party. In telling me about that, she told me about how she came to be locked up in juvenile hall for about 30 days.

TS: My mother, for some reason she thought the Black Panther Party was a cult, so she put me in juvenile hall. And I went to East Lake and then I went to Los Padrinos, and while I was in there I was recruitin' sisters to come into the party. So while I was in Los Padrinos, I had recruited three sisters, and our little ranks in terms of sisters began to grow.

TC: Wait a minute... You became a member of the Black Panther Party, your family felt that you had joined a cult and they put you in juvenile hall, and you ended up recruiting for the party out of the juvenile hall? Tell me about that.

TS: Well we had a program we used to call Each One Teach One. So when I came into the juvenile hall there was a lot of sisters there that was lost, misguided – reminded me of myself... Some places we had individual cells. But that same question to me was my question to the sisters: Do you know who you are? And I would tell them who they were historically. And I talked to them about – my name then was Linda, Linda Miles – and I said "and I'm a Black Panther." They wanted to know what a Black Panther was, and I started talkin' about the ten-point program, what our mission was – it was a non-violent organization but we believed in self defense by any means necessary. Historically, I told them: "Look, we were kings and queens in Africa. We came over the Middle Passage. Hundreds of thousands of us died in the Middle Passage." I talked about the plantation, I talked about the Emancipation Proclamation – this so-called thing Lincoln did to free the slaves that was not true. And I just went on and on about our history about what we need to do. And they said: "Can girls do it too?" When you become a Panther, you a Panther. You're not a girl, you're not a boy, you're a Panther. And the brothers gave us respect.

TC: And you was runnin' this to the sisters in the juvenile hall? And when I get out look me up. This is where I'm at?

TS: And they came. They came. And I was so surprised cause one, I felt like I could not reach her. It was three. A sister named Ethel, a sister named Stephanie. Audrey, Esley and Brenda Frank, they weren't in juvenile hall with me, but they had went to Fremont High School with me, and I had talked with them, so I had four sisters that came into the Black Panther Party under myself.

TC: As a student at Fremont High School, was there a Black Student Union at Fremont High School?

TS: It was not established till later when I had basically dropped out of school. When I dropped out of Fremont High School, it was because of what I had learned from the Black Panther Party, I became a straight A student just from the political education classes and reading and talking to other people, and my education in the community – I became a straight A student.

TC: What kind of grades were you makin' before that?

TS: Before I came to Fremont High School it was like a B average. When I came to Fremont High School, bein' honest, when I started lookin' at fine brothers and listening to jazz and hangin' out, them grades kinda dropped, you know? They really dropped.

TC: Kinda dropped? Kinda fell? One legged A's... the A with one leg... [Laughter]

TS: You know, bein' involved with the Black Panther Party, I increased my reading, I just started reading various genres, I talked to everybody, different cultures, I got involved with everything – Cesar Chavez's movement – everything. They had made me so politically aware to the point where I could hold meetings with doctors and lawyers and they would think I had a college education. I hadn't even finished high school. One day, one of the counselors came to me and they said: "You know what? I don't know what you're doin' but we can't teach you anything else and you should go on to college ahead of your class." So I took the GED. Then, we had grades like

A12, B12. I think I was in B12. They told me I need to take the GED and go on to college, cause I need to go on to college, and that's what I did. I went on to Los Angeles City College about six months before my class graduated.

TC: And eventually you went on, and I believe you got a Bachelor of Arts degree?

TS: In terms of my education, I have an AS degree in electronic engineering, a Bachelors in childhood development and a Masters in multicultural education, and I'm currently workin' on a PhD in holistic nutrition.

TC: At that time, based upon your work in the Black Panther Party and your exposure, you became a straight A student, and you have had an opportunity to teach children here in the Los Angeles school district.

TS: I'm currently a teacher now with LA Unified. I was a teacher for the 6th grade for two years and now I'm teaching 4th grade at a charter school in Los Angeles.

TC: Based upon your experiences as a student making grades and what you're seeing now, what would you say is the difference?

TS: There's a big difference. It's amazing, the difference, because when I was going to school, although I was hanging with the Panthers, I still valued education. I read. I was aware of what was going on around me and in my community, and I really don't find our children reading. And a lot of them have young mothers and fathers that are not reading. When I sent home an assignment, the children can't do it and their parents can't do it. It's really scary because I wonder, down the line, what is going to happen to our children.

TC: Our children are going to be fine if they continue to have teachers like Talibah Shakir. My name is Thandisizwe Chimurenga. You've been listening to *Some Of Us Are Brave*, a Black women's radio program.

I'll leave you in the words of Fred Hampton: "Let me say peace to you if you're willing to fight for it."

Geneva Reed-Veal

Twenty-eight-year old Sandra Bland was assaulted and wrongfully arrested on July 10, 2015, in Prairie View, Texas. Three days later, she was found hanging in the Waller County jail and her death was eventually ruled a suicide. Her mother, Geneva Reed-Veal, was approached briefly during the annual Oscar Grant Foundation banquet in Hayward, CA, on February 27, 2016.

• • •

Thandisizwe Chimurenga: I'm so sorry for your loss. I wanted to ask you one question: what is it that you want people to know?

Geneva Reed-Veal: About me? About Sandy? About the system and about how torn up it is? I want people to know that we are dealing with a broken justice system. My daughter is like so many others who is waiting for justice to occur. Up to this point, it's just us that's not getting it. And so, what I want the world to know is it's gonna take more than one race, more than one creed, more than one color. We all gonna have to get together, stand together, and make this thing change. We need an overhaul all across the country, and it's gonna take more than just Blacks, more than just whites, more than Chinese, more than Hispanics. All of that has to be melted together. That's when true change is gonna come.

TC: That's what you want people to know?

GRV: Yes, ma'am. Yes.

TC: Thank you so much.

Honorable Cynthia McKinney

The Honorable Cynthia McKinney is a former Congresswoman from Georgia, having served six terms in the United States House of Representatives. First elected in 1992, McKinney was the first African-American woman from Georgia to serve in Congress. She is also the former 2008 Green Party candidate for President of the United States. This interview was conducted in North Hollywood, California, on December 10, 2006.

• • •

Thandisizwe Chimurenga: First of all, I want to thank you so much for coming. Thank you so much for allowing me this opportunity to interview. I greatly appreciate the work that you've done. Thank you for everything that you have done. I want to thank you.

Cynthia McKinney: I get shy when people start saying "thank you." I get so much hate. I'm accustomed to the hate and it hardens you, but to get love, gosh, that's a whole new phenomenon.

TC: I know and I want to talk to you about that hate.

CMK: Okay.

TC: In this past year, in particular, you got absolutely no support from the Democratic Party, the people who were supposed to have your back. Whether it was the so-called Congressional Black Caucus or other Democrats. The first thing that I wanted to know was why did you continue to remain a part of the Democratic Party? Why didn't you leave and go become an independent, for example, especially after losing the primary in Georgia?

CMK: Georgia election laws are extremely limiting for candidates, and are particularly skewed toward the two parties or the three parties that have valid access in Georgia, which is the Democrats, Republicans, and the Libertarians. Any other political party is out of luck. I got a lot of emails from people who were suggesting that I should take the [Joe] Lieberman[1] route, because Lieberman showed that you could lose in a primary and then run as an independent. Then, after the election, he demonstrated that an independent could win. There are probably some lessons in the Lieberman experience, but I couldn't do that in Georgia, because Georgia law prevents a candidate who has lost in the primary from running as an independent. Georgia also has the open primary which allows the Republicans to cross over and to participate in the Democratic primary. That, of course, is what they have repeatedly done to me. The open primary statute can be used as the equivalent of the all-white primary, and it should be repealed as well. We've got a lot of work to do in Georgia.

TC: What message do you have for the Los Angeles area community, why are you here this weekend and what would you like us to know?

CMK: I'm here to do fundraisers for two community organizations. I think it's wonderful to be able to come to a place like Los Angeles. This is like the big city for me, and to make a contribution to people who are sometimes otherwise neglected. It's a good thing for activists to get together with other activists. With me being from the South, there are a lot of people in California who have roots in the South.

We reestablish a tie, and that's important too, but the thing that people in Los Angeles need to know is that, no matter how bad you might think it is in California, it's a whole lot worse in some other areas. Therefore, whatever the issues are that motivate the activists to stay active, please remain motivated because California is like a beacon for other parts of the country who have not yet progressed to the positions that you have, and have secured certain rights that you have. It's not as bad as you may think [laughs].

TC: Okay, I'll keep that in mind.

---

1 Joseph Lieberman (born 1942) served as a United States senator from Connecticut from 1989 to 2013. A former member of the Democratic Party, he was its nominee for Vice President in the 2000 U.S. presidential election. During his final term in office, he was officially listed as an independent Democrat.

CMK: Even with Schwarzenegger[2] [laughs].

TC: I saw *American Blackout*.[3] It was one of those films that really touched my heart and especially the part about the doors and the windows. A single mom, a Black woman, from the South, and you're out here battling and you get all of this madness that you already have been dealing with since 2001. Then the incident happens in March,[4] and my question to you is what is it that keeps you going? I know you talked about the fact of coming out here and being in solidarity with other activists, what is it that keeps you going?

CMK: I read a lot. I love to read. The statistics come out, whether it's *New York Times*, National Urban League, United for Fair Economy, Harvard University, Kaiser Family Foundation, Hall House, Loyola University, United States Department of Labor, all of the statistics tell us the same story. That is, that Black America is losing ground. If that's the case, then we have to do something about that. White America should not want there to be a chasm in this country such that the divisions can be so strong and so stark that we don't know each other. Certainly, a strong America can't sustain the kind of poverty, the kind of division, the racial gaps.

Dr. David Satcher's[5] most recent report came out and said that over 80,000 Black people died for no other reason than that they are Black. We already know from other studies that even if Blacks have the same health insurance as whites, they don't get the same health care. Therefore, they die sooner than they're supposed to. They live sicker lives than they're supposed to. This is something that makes me outraged. Then you add on top of it the blatant injustices and the misuse of taxpayers' money by this Bush

---

2 Arnold Schwarzenegger (born 1947) served as the Republican 38th governor of California between 2003 and 2011.
3 *American Blackout* (2006) is a documentary film directed by Ian Inaba. The film chronicles the 2002 defeat and 2004 reelection of Congresswoman Cynthia McKinney to the U.S. House of Representatives; it also discusses issues surrounding voter disenfranchisement and the use of voting machines..
4 On March 29, 2006, Representative Cynthia McKinney had a dispute with Capitol Police. McKinney entered a government building after walking around the metal detector at the security checkpoint. She was grabbed by a Capitol Police officer who stated that he had been calling after her "Ma'am, Ma'am!" Two days later, the officer filed a police report claiming that McKinney had "struck his chest with a closed fist." Members of Congress are not required to pass through metal detectors but they are asked to wear identifying lapel pins. The incident made headlines and sparked controversies over whether the officers present failed to recognize her as a Member of Congress because she was not wearing the appropriate lapel pin and whether McKinney had just cause to assert that racial profiling played a role in the incident.
5 David Satcher (1941-) is a physician and public health administrator. He was a four-star admiral in the U.S. Public Health Service Commissioned Corps and served as the 10th Assistant Secretary for Health, and the 16th Surgeon General. Satcher was appointed by Bill Clinton, and remained Surgeon General into George W. Bush's first term.

administration. It clearly tells us that we have to do something to save our country from these people or else we will not be able to save ourselves.

Mario Savio[6] said that there comes a time when the machine becomes so odious that you can't even take part. You have to put your entire body against the gears, and the levers, and the wheels of the machine, and you have to say to the owners that they have to stop it and if they don't stop it, we will stop it. Now, I take his words seriously. I think that this machine has reached the point where it is so odious that I can't even take part.

TC: Since I do work with *Some Of Us Are Brave* – I know that there are a lot of Black women who look to you, appreciate you, support you, were angry for you, had your back in whatever way they could, we do appreciate you. As a Black woman, what are you feeling right now? What message do you have for sisters here in Los Angeles?

CMK: My struggle is the struggle of Black women everywhere. Generalized women, but we're the ones who have the mortality gap, the infant-mortality gap, the family-income gap. Those statistics are all us. Nearly half of the men between the ages of 16 and 64 in New York City are unemployed. What does that mean for marriage, what does that mean for families, for the household? We have a particular struggle because of our color. I try to give voice to that because even though I've had advantages of my work, my job, and my parents, and all of that, my education, but at the end of the day, I'm still a Black woman who's trying to raise a son. My son could end up like Sean Bell.[7]

I don't have any advantage just because I served in the United States Congress. That didn't stop white police officers – I probably shouldn't say this it'll get me in trouble, but that didn't stop white police officers from saying that they didn't recognize me. It wasn't just in March. It was in January, it was in February, it was in March, it was the whole 12 years that I was in Congress. I had to deal with the fact that I'm a natural, proud, Black woman wearing Afrocentric clothes, who some people thought didn't belong on Capitol Hill.

---

6 Mario Savio (1942-1996) was an American activist and a key member of the Berkeley Free Speech Movement. In mid-1964, he joined the Freedom Summer projects in Mississippi and was involved in helping African-Americans register to vote. He also taught at a freedom school for Black children in McComb, Mississippi.

7 Sean Bell was shot and killed in 2006 in New York City, while unarmed, by NYPD police. Bell was killed on the morning before his wedding. He was 23 years old. In 2008, all three of the police officers involved were acquitted on all counts.

TC: Based on that, what's your message to sisters?

CMK: Sisters are strong, but we can't afford to get weak. We can't afford to be weak because our entire race really is dependent on us being strong. I know sometimes that bothers the brothers, but we support the brothers. Were it not for our strength, the brothers would be in an even more dire predicament. The Sean Bells, that doesn't just happen in New York. I'm sure that Los Angeles and the Ramparts Division had a lot of things going on in the Black community. From Los Angeles to New York City our plight is the same, but we have to withstand the daily indignities of being Black and struggle to make our country better, our community better so that our children can get the lives that they deserve to have.

TC: Thank you so much for your time.

CMK: Okay.

Janaya Khan

Janaya Khan is a co-founder of Black Lives Matter–Toronto, as well as a social justice theorist, activist and educator. They are now living in Los Angeles, California, where Janaya continues their work. This interview was conducted on March 10, 2016, for the Rootwork Edition of Uprising, *a morning drive time show, on KPFK-Pacifica Los Angeles.*

• • •

Thandisizwe Chimurenga: Last week on what was called Super Tuesday,[1] Donald Trump, "The Donald," walked away with about seven states under his belt. The other day he went to Michigan and Mississippi amongst some of the others. Donald Trump seems to be this unstoppable force that has got a lot of people shook. Like, "What are we gon do? I'm thinking about moving to Canada." I know a lot of folks are talking about that. Black people have tried that before though. Is that going to work for Black folks who might be feeling kinda shook?

Just the other night at a rally in North Carolina there were some protesters at a Trump rally. As they were being escorted out one of them was attacked, physically assaulted by a man in the audience and security arrested the protester. Not the man who assaulted him, but the Black protester. The white man with the ponytail, he was able to sit back down and enjoy the rally. What's that old saying is getting kinda hectic? It's been kinda hectic

---

1 Super Tuesday is the U.S. presidential primary election day in February or March when the greatest number of U.S. states hold primary elections and caucuses. The results on Super Tuesday are therefore a strong indicator of the likely eventual nominee of each political party.

for Black folk. The question is what are we going to do? While the rest of the country is using Google to research moving to Canada, while AlterNet and other independent publications are talking about moving to Canada, what does that mean for Black folks?

Should we try and make a run for it?

On the line with me now is Janaya Khan. They are an organizer, activist and social justice educator in Toronto, Ontario Canada, also a co-founder of Black Lives Matter–Toronto. I guess the fact that there is a Black Lives Matter in Toronto should answer the question, but we gon talk to Janaya anyway, are you there?

Janaya Khan: Yes, I am.

TC: Thank you so much for being on the show this morning. How you doing?

JK: I'm good. I'm good I'm happy to be here.

TC: Have you been hearing from Black folks who want to make that jump and come on up to Canada?

JK: More overwhelmingly so, it's been from white people. I think my favorite sort of story to speak to very quickly when I think about Americans migrating to Canada when things get really intense is Angela Davis.[2] She was speaking at York University a few years ago. York University is in Toronto. She said, "You know, I used to think when things got really bad in the States and as you know they got really bad for me. That I would come to Canada and I would escape to Canada when they did." And then she's like, "But then I came here and now I know better."

TC: What did she see?

JK: So here's the thing, if we just look at it from a couple of standpoints. The United States has 300 million-and-something people in it. Canada has about 35 million people in it even though the landmass is 1.1 percent larger than the United States. So we don't have a huge population of people. And that's going to inform what we understand about histories of resistance. It's going to inform what we understand about populations and what those implications are. And so, if we're looking at Canada right now, of that

---
2 See note on Angela Davis on page 26.

35 million or so only 2.9 percent are Black. But we represent 10 percent of the Canadian federal inmate population. And what she was speaking to when she came down there was the reality of anti-Black racism. Though maybe perhaps not as widespread because Black people are not everywhere in Canada in huge numbers. But in a very focused form of anti-Black racism that is simultaneously erased and denied.

TC: Simultaneously erased?

JK: And denied. What I mean by that is Canada's history of slavery, of its colonial past has been erased from its memory. Canada is a country where the histories of enslavement extend back three centuries, 300 years. That extends beyond French and English periods because of course Canada was colonized by both. Enslavement of African peoples was integral to the functioning of Canadian society and so you learn about …

TC: Let me cut you off for a minute. Let me cut you off because now I'm confused. Black folks were trying to get to Canada. We were just trying to get North to get free.

JK: Right

TC: In terms of here in the US; so what do you mean the history of enslavement in Canada?

JK: I mean it's extensive and that's it, right? We're talking about a narrative where it's "you go North to get free." So for one, while Canada may have in certain areas abolished slavery first, but doesn't mean that enslavement didn't exist for 300 years and, while you might have some settlements like in Africville,[3] for example, in Halifax and between 1840 and 1860, for example – just because there was some free settlements in that area doesn't mean that the rest of the country was also enacting freedom for Black people.

Then also you need to consider when it comes to freedom and what that means in a place like Canada where you have rampant anti-Black racism or

---

[3] Africville was a small community located in Halifax, Nova Scotia. It existed from the early 1800s to the 1960s. Africville was founded by Black Nova Scotians from a variety of origins. Many of the first settlers were formerly enslaved African Americans and Black Loyalists who were freed by the Crown during the American Revolutionary War and War of 1812. Throughout the 20th century, Halifax neglected the community, failing to provide basic infrastructure and services. During the late 1960s, the City of Halifax condemned the area, demolishing houses and relocating residents.

you have major areas and provinces that still enforce enslavement; where you still have histories of the KKK ... the question really then is free to what? Let's look at Africville, for example. That's an important part of Black Canadian history. Again, I don't really encourage Black Americans especially to come to Canada and not have an investment in that Black Canadian history because there will be a very rude awakening.

Where you have a settlement there, a free settlement, Black people are building off of freedoms, folks who are searching for freedom, who came to the North, ended up in Halifax and built this wonderful area that was eventually systematically destroyed by the city. Nova Scotia was the last stop on the Underground Railroad.[4] That's where Halifax is. If you watch a national television propaganda that comes up, it'll show a bunch of like, "Happy enslaved people popping out of furniture and finding new life in the Great White North."

TC: No, not the happy darkies! No, they don't do that, do they?!

JK: Yeah, right?! And not everybody knows what a horrendous time some former African-American enslaved people and their descendants had on the East Coast. Part of that history is in Africville, where local governments, it started to provide such amenities: it started to provide water and electricity and snow plowing, and then they decided that this was actually land that they could use. I'm not talking about the 1800s where they decided to demolish a place where Black people congregated. This happened in 1964, right?

They wanted to redevelop Africville for industry so they kicked out poor Black people and erased that history despite the resiliency of those locals. This city built a hospital for diseased World War II soldiers right nearby in their neighborhood. They put a toxic waste dump on the other side and they eventually put a railroad right through the area. The only thing that exists from Africville is a monument. Out of an entire settlement and another entire community, and in one of the areas that sort of symbolized the last stop in the Underground Railroad. The only thing that stands right there right now is a monument.

---

4 The Underground Railroad was a secret network of individuals and safe houses in the United States during the 19th century. Its purpose was to help enslaved African Americans escape from slavery and reach free states or Canada, where slavery was abolished. The Underground Railroad operated from the late 18th century until the Civil War in the 1860s.

And that I think is a really great example of what Canada's relationships to Black people are. It's one of erasure. It's one of denial. It's one of very, very serious insidious and pervasive anti-Black racism.

TC: My world is being rocked this morning. My vision of Canada as a haven, a safe haven, is being torn to shreds. I don't think Janaya cares and that's bothering me. Janaya, what are you – Listen –

JK: [Laughter]

TC: Listen, Okay, Janaya check this out, right? What about Canada's new Prime Minister Justin Trudeau? I'm hearing all these wonderful glowing things about him. He look kinda cute. He kinda young. What's the dealio?

JK: [Laughter] What's the dealio? Do you remember when Obama first came to office?

TC: Yes, I do.

JK: 2008 and he rode the "Hope train" and he's just liberal dude, good-looking, he's charming. Eventually, he spoke to us through a social media platform. Well, if you look at the histories of Canada and United States and our relationships. When you had George Bush, we had Stephen Harper. We had Stephen Harper for a little while longer, unfortunately. Because here's another thing that's really interesting, there's no cap for how long we can have a prime minister. In the U.S., a president can be in power for two terms. In Canada, the prime minister can be empowered indefinitely if he continues to be voted in. Harper had the longest run as a Prime Minister – I think 11 years – since the early 1900s.[5] When Harper was around Bush was around, and the two of them were actually pretty good friends. Now, we have Obama in his last couple of months and we have Justin Trudeau coming in, there's the moment when the two of them are relating to each other, they're making jokes about hockey and who has the best team and all these other things. I'm thinking wow, well, actually as per usual, right? We're just right behind the United States, we sort of follow in particular trends.

So now, we have this liberal progressive prime minister who is significantly better than Stephen Harper like Obama was considered significantly

---

5 Mackenzie King served for 21 years split into three non-consecutive terms, starting in 1921. His third term lasted 13 years and ended in 1948. Pierre Trudeau served 15 years in two separate terms, starting in 1968 and ending in 1984. Stephen Harper served 9 years and 271 days but it seemed longer.

better than George Bush, but what fundamentally did Obama change for Black people in terms of police brutality? I'm talking about before these last few months that he's in power is start to make some very interesting and necessary choices around naming mass incarceration but we're talking about before that.

When I think about Justin Trudeau, I think he's going to make some changes on foreign policy. He's not necessarily going to be like Stephen Harper where he's going to allow fighter jets to also get involved in Iran and Syrian relations to support the United States. He withdrew those jets and in that way we're going to look at Justin Trudeau as someone who was much more progressive, much more present. He calls himself a feminist. He cries about Indigenous relations and how Aboriginal people are treated as he calls folks in Canada. What does that tend to retain for Indigenous people?

We're talking about a country who historically voted against water as a basic fundamental human right because that would require providing irrigation systems for people living on reserves, Indigenous people in Canada. We're talking about a government that sent body bags and slop pails when irrigation systems were requested on reserves.

TC: Body bags?

JK: That's correct. And slop pails.

TC: Body bags as in terms of where to put people who have died?

JK: That's correct.

TC: Yeah. I'm not feeling Canada right about now. I'm not feeling Canada.

JK: It's more than just a myth of a haven, it's the myth of the racial haven, right? That's really what it is. When I think about that, I'm like, "Okay, I think Trudeau is going to force the conversation that a lot of Black people in America, unfortunately, had to go through," which is like "but we gave you a Black president, doesn't that mean racism is over?" I wonder because I know that that offended and angered so many American people, Black American people especially, and why they wouldn't ask the same questions of a place like Canada is partly informed by being convinced that the States is one of the worst and best places to live in the world.

Canada has always, always, always, has always been the option but the reality of living in Canada is very, very different. I mean in Toronto, police have just been granted a huge boost in their financial structure so that they now have assault rifles and that is a direct result of Black Lives Matter–Toronto and the work that we've been doing there. We now have police officers on the street who have assault rifles. We're talking about a place where without our organizing on the ground "carding," which is a campaign that has been happening in Toronto and Greater Toronto Area for decades, has allowed police to arbitrarily stop and search and arbitrarily retain the information of anyone that they suspect.

Now, because of anti-Black racism, which in fact very much exists in Canada, you have Black people who are being three to four times more likely to be "carded" than anyone else. Now, keep in mind that the "carding" practice directly coincides with the fact in the last ten years, there's been an 80 percent increase of African-Canadians being streamlined to Canadian federal prison. We make up 2.9 percent of the population but we represent ten percent of the Canadian federal inmate population. Those numbers are astronomical. The reality is the majority of those arrests are happening in Ontario and specifically in Toronto, where the largest population of Black people in Canada exists.

TC: You said "carding" is the Canadian equivalent of stop and frisk, three to four times more likely to be "carded"?

JK: More likely to be carded. Any other population of people; not in this particular moment it's been suspended because of the pushback that we've done on the ground but really they're going to just reinvent it and rearticulate it in a way. Canada I think is in a really scary time where we've become a prison state in so many ways where the investment is in developing prisons, and when you expand prisons, you create a need and a demand for bodies to serve them. It has been Black and Indigenous bodies that fill Canadian federal prisons.

I want to draw attention to something as well, because I think this is really important. One of the times when Canada's racist history and colonizing past was about to come to the forefront, something significant happened in American history. There's something called "starlight tours" that happened and used to, I think still do in certain cases but it happened a lot in Saskatchewan.

What is a "starlight tour"? It's when the RCMP – which is the Royal Canadian Mounted Police – would pick up an inebriated Indigenous person; someone who was very drunk, and they would drive them to the outskirts of the city, make sure they had no exterior clothing – it's in the middle of winter; they don't have a winter jacket or anything else – and leave them there. A legend was starting to be created because no one could understand why all these Indigenous people were freezing to death on the outskirts of town when they very much knew how to get home, when they knew the places where they live very well, when they were really great at navigation.

And so just as the UN got involved and the whole world was starting to try to turn its eyes to Canada and think about the horrors of something called the "starlight tours" it was happening so frequently that it was becoming an urban legend, 9/11 happened. As soon as 9/11 happened, the story changed in what was going to be on the national/international stage on Canada's colonizing task. The world became concerned and familiar with 9/11 and all the implications of that disaster.

Let's give another example, because the reality is, the connections between Canada and the United States in terms of treatment of Black people are consistent.

The differences and the reason why we don't hear about it as much is one, from population and two, because of American egocentrism. And what we know in Canada is the more Black people that exist in Canada, the more obvious and apparent that racism and that erasure is. Like in the 1960s when Canada had its racist immigration policy and wouldn't allow Caribbean Black people to enter unless they were domestic workers. So there's a whole generation of Black people who are the result of those particular racist policies. Or like in 1969 when you had the Computer Riots.

And the Computer Riots were about Black Caribbean people coming into Montreal to go to school. Of course, again, the more Black people that are in Canada, the more obvious anti-Black racism is. There was a professor there who was very obvious in his racism against Black folks. He would alter grades to suit his purposes and needs. Even if the work was identical, Black people would find that they were still being marked less. They called him on this and the professor denied it. It was six students who were all Black who said this is happening, and it got to the point where a lot of people rallied behind these folks to talk about racism in Canada, in general, in Montreal in 1969.

It's called the Computer Riot because back then a computer or two could take up an entire room, and somebody set one of those floors, one of those computer rooms on fire. Evidence suggests that it was a police officer who set that on fire, but more specifically, evidence suggests that it was a Black person in the States who had been recruited by the FBI and the CIA under COINTELPRO and sent to Canada to be an infiltrator. To be a part of those particular movements and spy on what they thought was a Black Panther Party being developed in Montreal in 1969.

So when you think about something like that – and, by the way, there's a great documentary on that called *The Ninth Floor* that just came out and has been circulating. They talk about the connection between those histories and what bodies of security were working together in Canada and the United States so that the connection was made very seamlessly; that there's always been concern of Black Power movements in Canada. Let's fast-forward a little bit. Just a few days ago, it was the 25th year since the Rodney King[6] beating. Now, that was one of the great catalysts of our time.

Before the age of body cameras on police, whenever they do have them – if they're not technically malfunctioning at the exact moment when terrible things are happening. Before the age of cellphones, a neighbor was able to videotape Rodney King being beaten by four white police officers with batons while he was on the ground defenseless. Even with that video footage, all four white officers were acquitted. Now, Canada had a solidarity protest, in solidarity with Rodney King, in 1994. This is important, because the Black Action Defense Committee has had huge histories in Canada. Specifically in Toronto around fighting for Black rights.

When that happened, about two days before the protest, another Black person, Raymond Constantine Lawrence, was shot twice in the chest by Toronto police. While there was a solidarity rally for King it also became about Raymond Constantine Lawrence and also, the eight other Black

---

6 Rodney King was an African-American man whose beating by police officers in Los Angeles in 1991 was captured on video. After the incident, four LAPD officers were charged with assault with a deadly weapon and use of excessive force. However, in 1992, a jury acquitted the officers of all charges. King passed away in 2012 at the age of 47.

people who had been murdered and shot by Toronto police in the last four years. You might think, "Eight Black people in four years well it's not as bad as the United States." Then again, you have to look at population differences.

With that happening, that history of resistance that is more often one-sided than not. Black Canada are showing up in solidarity for Black Americans but Black Americans are not showing up for solidarity in Canada. There's reasons why for that. Part of it is U.S. egocentrism. Part of it is because the stories aren't actually told. Why would American media pick up on it? So who's telling those stories, and who gets to access them? Especially when Canada barely covers it, Canadian media barely covers it itself because it's so deeply invested in being the good whites: "We're not as bad as the United States." That is a myth that has become enshrined in Canada and is one of the most loathsome and insidious of them, but, let's go back to the story.

While the LA riots are happening in Los Angeles, the Yonge Street Riots are happening in Toronto at pretty much the exact same time. Yonge Street is the longest street in Canada and it is also in a very concentrated area in downtown. It's also one of the most affluent. Black protesters who were fighting for Rodney King and fighting for Raymond Lawrence started protesting in front of the U.S. Consulate, marching to City Hall, were denied entry and then took over Yonge street, burned things, looted the things and all those narratives around, "Black people always turn on their own communities." Yonge Street definitely was not our own community.

And I purposely name it riots, instead of uprisings. We saw burning happen and we saw the police who didn't have any idea what to do with all these protesters. Eventually, they got on horses with batons and ended up beating up a whole bunch of folks and about 30 people were arrested. The histories of, just in LA and Toronto for example, is something that's incredibly necessary because if you think about the fact that we had a solidarity rally then. And then you fast forward, you fast forward all the way into 2014, when Mike Brown[7] was killed and then we have the court case and Darren Wilson, and the world knows that he's going to be acquitted. That you're going to get no indictment.

---

7 On August 9, 2014, 18-year-old Michael Brown was shot and killed by police officer Darren Wilson in Ferguson, Missouri, a suburb of St. Louis. This was followed by several waves of protests.

We aren't even Black Lives Matter–Toronto yet. We're a group of Black people who know how necessary it is to show solidarity. But also like our predecessors, we named Mike Brown in what happened but we also used it to connect back to the murder of Jermaine Carby, a 33-year-old Black man who had been killed only a month or two before by Peel police. Peel is right outside of Toronto. We talked about Jermaine Carby, we had a relative of his come out and speak. What we know is Jermaine Carby's hands were up when he was shot several times. His hands were up; the autopsy shows that.

That story being connected, linked to Mike Brown, is incredibly important because the same narratives came up, the same villifying in the media; the dehumanizing in the media, where you have no indictments in the court and public indictments of our Black people happening in the media. We had a protest that brought out over 3000 people who showed up for that. The next year after that we had Andrew Loku,[8] when we're connecting Andrew Loku to Freddie Gray,[9] and we're talking about Sandra Bland.[10] And then a Black transwoman died out here and we made those connections as well because, when a Black transwoman who does sex work dies in Toronto, it doesn't need to be directly at the hands of the police so much so that, so much is the fact that sex work has not been decriminalized in Toronto. The necessary safety networks that could possibly exist because the police are also something that sex-working people have to be afraid of, have to be concerned about. That infrastructure isn't there and so we're making those connections.

From that protest in 2014, you have Black Lives Matter–Toronto was born and around the same times were Black Lives Matters chapters across the United States were popping up.

TC: Janaya, I'm sorry. We're getting short on time here. I would love to hear more about it. Even though you're breaking my heart and rocking

---

[8] In July 2015, Andrew Loku was shot dead by Toronto police. Andrew's death raised troubling questions about police response to people experiencing mental health crises, as well as the intersection of race and mental health issues, as a disproportionate number of individuals experiencing mental health crises shot by Toronto police are Black.

[9] In April 2015, Freddie Gray, a 25-year-old African-American, was arrested by the Baltimore Police Department over what former prosecutor Marilyn Mosby claimed was his legal possession of a knife. While in police custody Gray sustained fatal injuries.

[10] Sandra Bland was a 28-year-old African-American woman who was found hanged in a jail cell in Waller County, Texas, on July 13, 2015, three days after being arrested during a traffic stop. Officials found her death to be a suicide. There were protests against her arrest, disputing the cause of death, and alleging racial violence against her.

my world. I would love to hear more about the reality of Black folks in Canada. Real quick, what's next up in terms of calendar items for Black Lives Matter–Toronto? If you can tell us real quick.

JK: Yes, yes. We have a freedom school to be launched in the summertime. We are fundraising for the development of resources and infrastructure for our freedom school, such a very important thing that's happening. The next major thing that's happening is interestingly enough Pride Toronto, which has been historically white and historically anti-Black, elected to have Black Lives Matter–Toronto as their honored group. That's a very loaded thing considering what Pride has become, but at Black Lives Matter–Toronto, we're very much invested in turning it into something very radically different. It has been in the last two years and bringing that to those radical and political routes around Black and trans people.

TC: Okay. If people want more information on what you are doing. How they can keep up with you, where can they get that information?

JK: If you want to get in touch with Black Lives Matter–Toronto it's at Blacklivesmatterto@gmail.com.

TC: I've been speaking with Janaya Khan, a social educator and activist based in Toronto, Ontario. Co-founder of Black Lives Matter–Toronto, who just broke my heart, rocked my world. Basically told me I can't flee to Canada when Donald Trump wins so I might have to look for some other place. But I appreciate you anyway, Janaya, so much for the work that you are doing.

JK: [Laughter] If you want to come to Canada, just remember that we're cute in "The Six." I'm saying, we're cuter than Jamaica. If you want to come [laughter] to kick it, we totally support that. We're down.

TC: I just can't stay [laughter]. Thank you so much Janaya. Appreciate you and all that you do. Thank you for being on the show.

JK: Thanks for having me.

Kadiatou Diallo

Kadiatou Diallo is the mother of Amadou Diallo, murdered by the New York Police Department on February 4, 1999. In May 2003 her memoir My Heart Will Cross This Ocean: My Story, My Son, Amadou *was published by One World/Random House. In June 2003 Mrs. Diallo travelled to Los Angeles for a book signing at Leimert Park's Eso Won Bookstore. Although she spoke with* Some of Us Are Brave *members Sherrie Ross, Ayana Canada and myself earlier in the day at KPFK studios, neither the audio or a transcript of that interview are available. I caught up with Mrs. Diallo after the book signing to ask her some brief, general questions about women in Guinea.*

• • •

Thandisizwe Chimurenga: You spoke with us earlier and you talked about the relationships between men and women in Guinea. You talked about how women were very independent prior to the coming of Islam. You talked about how that changed when Islam came, but the Quran talks about the equality of men and women. That there is no dominance, there's nothing in the Quran that says men should dominate women and how men have used the Quran to dominate women. I wanted to ask you about what is happening in Guinea in terms of the relationships between men and women. Are there still spheres of influence where women have control, are there women's societies, what is it like for a woman today in Guinea?

Kadiatou Diallo: Well, women today in Guinea are well organized. They're organized in a community level and state level. You have women as doctors, as teachers, as spiritual peers for their children and their sisters. And they're a leading example in the society in Guinea. Whether it is in the rural area, in the village or in the city, women are the centerpiece of every family. But the relationship that I mentioned about, between men and women, was that they use the Quran to get back the power that the women have so much of, and they use it to explain to the women that Quran preaches to obey them. But women, as it is, in Guinea, we have ministers in the cabinet, in the government, we have women as pilots and university teachers. So it's civilized, and we have a civilization that is still ongoing. The practices of dominating women in the village were happening in the old days, 600, 700 years ago, but now it has changed tremendously.

TC: The other thing that I wanted to ask you about was, in terms of the spirituality and the healing that goes on, there's a belief that once you become Muslim you're supposed to do away with things of your culture that may not be Islamic, for example, and I know that in Africa there seems to be a peaceful coexistence between indigenous ways or certain indigenous beliefs and Islam. And I wanted to ask you about them in terms of your experiences in Guinea?

KD: We don't teach about religion in school, where we co-exist with the Christians. But the huge numbers of Muslim people make us the majority. We are over 90% Muslim in the country. But we do not have Islamic control in the system or an Islamic mentality. We believe that the connection between us and God depends on the spiritual level of every individual. So we don't have this type of problem that is happening elsewhere especially in the Arab countries.

TC: In other words like an Islamic state, that's not what Guinea is?

KD: No, That's not what it is. And I can give you one example, our head of state Lansana Conté[1] had two wives, he's married to two women. One is Christian, the first wife, and the second is Muslim. And the president is Muslim himself. So we don't have the Islamic domination in this typical situation that you see nowadays in the Arabic society. We don't have that

---

1 Lansana Conté (1934-2008) was a military official who served as the second President of Guinea, from 1984 until his death in December 2008.

in Guinea. It's totally different, it's independent. It's only the culture that we talk about but on a political level, we don't have that type of situation in Guinea.

TC: You also mentioned when I asked a question regarding what happened when Amadou was returned to Guinea and you said how if there was a murder or someone were killed, the family of the victim and the family of the perpetrator would gather at the mosque to pray and ask for forgiveness. Is that something that has happened since the arrival of Islam in Guinea or is that an adaptation or a new twist on something that you've done all along in terms of, over here we would call it "restorative justice," bringing the victim and the perpetrator together? I'm just wondering in terms of, in Guinea is that something that happened with the rise of Islam or is that something that has always been a way of life?

KD: It was the way of life. We were very organized even before the scholars came with their religion. You know, we have kingdoms, we have something like a constitution, the imam is the king of the village and he changes power every two years to a different one. Whatever happened, if something went wrong, like a crime is committed, the king is the one who can gather everyone under a big giant tree and then counsel the people to curb jealousy and then talk between people who have problems between them. So it is a way of life even before the religion, but because of the religion, we found now that everything is easier to be solved in the mosque because people come together at the mosque for prayers and then they stay there to solve problems. And at a spiritual level, we have the spiritual leaders who are believed to be like a saint, who would not tolerate any injustice, will not accept lies to be told. So these are the leading examples, the imams, and the spiritual leaders.

TC: Are there women spiritual leaders in Guinea or is that encouraged?

KD: You know, it's funny because …

TC: I know I told you two questions but I keep thinking of more.

KD: Let me tell you something, women are not involved in the mosque so much than to help clean the mosque and you know, organize how we can pray in the mosque. But every time we have to elect an imam for the mosque, women will vote because women are the ones who would be asked if the imam is a very good man. If he cannot fornicate, he cannot tell lies or he cannot do bad things. So women are very present and contribute a lot in electing an imam and also taking him off power if he misbehaves to the society. So it's well organized.

TC: Thank you so much for your time and your patience. I really appreciate it.

KD: Thank you very much and it was always nice talking with you. Yes.

TC: Thank you.

Medusa

On July 8, 2010, Johannes Mehserle was convicted of involuntary manslaughter in the death of 22-year-old Oscar Grant on January 1, 2009 in Oakland, California. After the verdict, hundreds gathered to protest in Los Angeles' Leimert Park, the cultural center of LA's African-American community. Leimert Park resident Medusa, a well-respected independent hip hop artist known as the "Gangsta Goddess" and "Godmother of West Coast Hip Hop," was observed entering the park and was asked for a comment for KPFK Evening News.

• • •

Medusa: What's going on, man.

Thandisizwe Chimurenga: How you doing?

M: Man, my heart hurts right now.

TC: Why your heart hurting right now?

M: You know, because I have held a gun and I've held a taser gun, and I know the difference. I know what it looks like looking down the barrel of both. And there's no way that a professional man that's used to handling those two different pieces of armory didn't know the difference. And, plus, he wasn't in a situation that was detrimental. This man's face was down so he had plenty of time to see and feel the difference and for him to just get involuntary manslaughter when it was obviously voluntary?

In addition to only getting two to four years? That means, that truly means he's only gonna get 18 months plus whatever time served because we know how it works. So the audacity for you to play on our intelligence, and to play with our feelings when they know that this is a prominent time for people to revolt. And this is a prime example of it. But I thank God that it's not a violent revolt and its contained and organized. See, we do that too. So my heart hurts for all of those many reasons.

TC: Thank you.

M: All right.

Michelle Alexander

Michelle Alexander is the author of the critically acclaimed The New Jim Crow: Mass Incarceration in the Age of Colorblindness. *The book was briefly banned in New Jersey state prisons in December of 2017. She spoke at Pasadena's Huntington Library on March 23, 2011 and this brief interview was conducted for* Some Of Us Are Brave.

• • •

Thandisizwe Chimurenga: I'd like to thank you for giving me these few minutes. I know you're tired, I know everybody wants to talk to you, so I really appreciate this.

Michelle Alexander: Well no, I'm very happy to be here and thrilled that so many people turned out, and that people were interested in talking about how we build a movement against mass incarceration. And that fills me with hope, so it gives me a little energy to carry on to the next stop.

TC: And I wanted to ask you about that, because you mentioned it in your book, and you talked about it tonight – the fact that you believe that only a social movement will get us out of this mess that we're in. But in your book, you talk about the fact that we went into the phase of lawyers, "taking over the struggle." And I was wondering if you could, for audio purposes, elaborate on that, you're saying that the problem is that the lawyers have taken over, and now we've gotten away from organizing and mobilizing, is that correct?

MA: Yes. You know, after the death of Martin Luther King and Malcolm X, civil rights advocacy became professionalized. And the lawyers did take over, and in litigating cases, and administrating consent decrees, and in lobbying behind closed doors for remedies and reforms. The movement ended and the work of civil rights advocacy became increasingly disconnected from the people the lawyers claim to represent. And I think we need to go back and pick up where Martin Luther King Jr. left off, and recommit ourselves to movement-building work, the building of a human rights movement on behalf of poor people of all colors. A movement for schools not jails; jobs not jails, and dismantle the system of incarceration and build a new system that values people of all colors, and invest in them and their communities.

TC: Let me ask you two questions that I have that are related to that thread. You talked about the fact that the phenomenon of mass incarceration that we are seeing and experiencing now: the seeds of it were planted during the Civil Rights movement. Can you tell me about that?

MA: Yes. If you wanted to trace the origins of the get-tough rhetoric that gave rise to the current war on drugs, it traces back to segregationists and former segregationists during the Civil Rights Movement who were groping for, searching for, formally colorblind language and rhetoric that would appeal to people in the south still committed to segregation, and they found that once it became no longer acceptable to say, "Segregation forever," they could say, "Law and order," and still appeal to those poor and working class whites, in particular, who are threatened by the Civil Rights Movement, and were hoping to reassert some control over the African-American population.

TC: The other question I wanted to ask you, in your research, had you come across any data to suggest not a mass incarceration, but certain individuals who were activists who fought against the type of ills that our communities suffer, who were part of the Civil Rights Movement and later the Black Power Movement – how they had been targeted for incarceration, political imprisonment, the targeting of political activists? Where does that figure in this phenomenon of mass incarceration that we see?

MA: As Hank Jones[1] mentioned earlier today, the Civil Rights Movement didn't just die – it was killed. And there was an organized effort to stop the movement and to ensure that it fell apart and disintegrated. And so it didn't just fall apart on its own. It was the result of FBI Cointel programs in an effort to dismantle that movement. And we're still paying the price for the end of that movement. And today I think we'd all be a lot better off if the spirit of that movement had remained alive and that those who were leaders in that movement were helping to guide the birth of a new movement today.

TC: Now, yet and still, you still encourage activism unlike the young man who advocated revolution in spite of that threat of dismantlement, of disruption by the federal government, you still encourage freedom fighting, as you call it.

MA: Oh, absolutely. I mean, there's no question that once this movement to end mass incarceration really begins to gain steam that many efforts will be made to stop it and to squelch it. And we just need to be prepared for that and be willing to act with as much bravery and courage as the freedom fighters and those who fought for liberation did to end slavery and to end Jim Crow. We've got to be willing to shake off our fear and our shame.

[Individuals surrounding our location are talking loudly and laughing.]

TC: Could you finish the last point you were just saying, please?

MA: Just that efforts will certainly be made to squelch the movement as it grows and gains steam, but we've got to be willing to act with bravery and courage, and follow in the footsteps of the abolitionists who fought to end slavery and those who've risked their lives to end Jim Crow. Nothing less than that sort of bravery and courage is required today. So we can't be discouraged in advance by the risk that someone may try to stop us.

TC: Thank you so much for your time.

MA: Thank you.

---

1 Hank Jones was a member of the Southern California Chapter of the Black Panther Party in Los Angeles, CA. He was one of eight men charged with the 1971 murder of a San Francisco police officer after the case was reopened in January of 2007. The men became known as the San Francisco 8. The case had originally been thrown out in 1975 when it was revealed that several of the men had been tortured into confessing to the 1971 murder. Charges against Jones and four others were dropped in July 2009.

Nisa Islam Muhammad

Nisa Islam Muhammad has been a print and broadcast journalist for 40 years and a staff writer for The Final Call *newspaper for 25 years. The* Final Call, *published by Min. Louis Farrakhan[2] and the Nation of Islam,[3] is the only Black weekly print newspaper in the United States. Recorded April 5, 2010, in Hawthorne, California.*

• • •

Thandisizwe Chimurenga: I'm sitting here with Sister Nisa Islam Muhammad, staff writer for *The Final Call* newspaper. How are you doing today, sister?

Nisa Islam Muhammad: I am doing wonderful. Thank you so much for having me.

TC: So the reason why I wanted to talk with you is because ... I've seen your name for a while now as a writer in *The Final Call* and a few other places where I've seen you publish. And then one day I looked up and I said "She done interviewed Assata?!" So let me ask you ... first of all, how is it that you went to Cuba?

NIM: I went to Cuba with a group of Black journalists organized by

---
2 Louis Farrakhan (1933-) heads the Nation of Islam (NOI). He was appointed National Representative of the Nation of Islam by Elijah Muhammad. In October 1995, he organized and led the Million Man March in Washington, D.C.
3 The Nation of Islam (NOI) is a religious and political organization founded in the United States by Wallace Fard Muhammad in 1930.

DeWayne Wickham.[1] DeWayne is good about taking Black journalists to places where they normally would not go, because usually they work for small newspapers or small organizations that don't have the resources and budgets to allow their reporters to go to across country to different places. So he organized a trip that was funded, I think, through Fannie Mae[2] or Freddie Mac;[3] he had to get sponsors, then we went to Cuba. And it was an incredible experience. We were there for a week. We had a tour of different spots in Cuba so that we could have an understanding of what was really going on in Cuba without the filtering that American media does. So we were able to see right off, on the ground, what was going on in the healthcare system, the education, the people, what they really think about Americans, what they really think about Fidel Castro,[4] their president, how they love him, the whole Cuba, the myth, so to speak, of what it's like to be in Cuba. It was just a great experience.

TC: Now, what year was this?

NIM: 2002.

TC: Now, you said you have taken two trips to Cuba?

NIM: That was my first trip. And I went back again in 2004. And I was sent there by Minister Farrakhan to do an extensive story on the medical school that is there, because the medical school there under the direction of President Fidel Castro is offering scholarships for Black and low-income students to come to Cuba and go to medical school for free. So we wanted to do a story, the Minister wanted me to do a story on that so that we could let people know that these medical school scholarships are available.

TC: I remember hearing about that, when that first happened. Now, to your knowledge, the scholarships are still available, and are people still taking advantage of it?

---

1 DeWayne Wickham (born 1946) is Dean Emeritus and founding dean of Morgan State University's School of Global Journalism & Communication and a founding member of the National Association of Black Journalists (NABJ).
2 The Federal National Mortgage Association (FNMA), commonly known as Fannie Mae, is a United States government-sponsored enterprise (GSE) and, since 1968, a publicly traded company created to expand the secondary mortgage market by securitizing mortgage loans in the form of mortgage-backed securities.
3 The Federal Home Loan Mortgage Corporation (FHLMC), commonly known as Freddie Mac, is a publicly traded, government-sponsored enterprise (GSE) created in 1970 to expand the secondary market for mortgages in the U.S.
4 Fidel Castro (1926-2016) led Cuba from 1959 until 2008. Castro was one of the key figures in the Cuban Revolution, which overthrew the U.S.-backed government of Fulgencio Batista in 1959.

NIM: Yes, the scholarships are still available, if anyone is interested in going to medical school and they have not been able to get into a medical school in the U.S. because there's limited spots, that there are there's a spot available for you in Cuba to go to medical school, where you will graduate without the debt, without the loans, without the "Oh my god, what am I going to do? I got to work so hard to pay off this money." You will graduate stress-free. And in fact, some of the recent graduates from the Cuban medical school were then sent to Haiti to work with the people in Haiti after the earthquake.

TC: Now, I just want to check to be sure because this was 2004 ... the second time that you went back and you did a story on this, this is now 2010. Still available?

NIM: It is still available. And for Women's International Day in Washington DC at the Cuban Interests Section – they don't have an embassy there – I met two young ladies who had recently graduated from the Cuban Medical School. And in fact, they were in Haiti, helping the people there after the earthquake. And so they shared their experiences. They loved it. Now, it's not like going to medical school in California. Let me, let me just warn your listeners. It's Cuba that has a 50-plus year embargo by the US. They're a poor country, but they make the best out of what they have. The dormitories are renovated military barracks. And so if you're looking for your own separate dorm where you have your own separate bathroom, don't go to Cuba. Don't embarrass yourself, because they're very rudimentary conditions, but you will get a first class medical education for free. So it's a trade-off.

But the trade-off is well worth the experience. Another thing is that you have to learn Spanish. So maybe for the first year there will be Spanish lessons because the classes are all taught in Spanish. All of the patients you will be working with speak Spanish, and so it's important to understand and know the language, but it's a great experience. And so yes, the scholarships are still available. Any of your listeners that are interested can contact Pastors for Peace, which is an organization in New York that is helping to administer the scholarships.

TC: Pastors for Peace, okay, Rev. Lucius Walker. Now, you stated that recently for Women's Day, which was March 8, the Cuban Interests

Section had a program and you were able to meet two sisters, two Black women, who had most recently been in Haiti, providing assistance because they were doctors, did they talk about their experiences? Can you share some of that?

NIM: They talked about their experiences, and they talked about how everything that they had learned specifically in medical school about compassion and love for people in need, that they were able to implement.

TC: Hold on, hold on, hold on. Okay, let's back up for a second. These were students in medical school, who's supposed to be learning anatomy and all "this that and the other." You said, compassion and love for people? Is that what you said?

NIM: It's a different experience. Yes, they learn compassion, they learn love, it's so it's not about a dollar. It's not about who can pay because in Cuba, medical services are free. So then what's the incentive to be a doctor if the services are free? The incentives are compassion and love for humankind and for the well-being of your patients. And so this is what they learned: they learned how to serve people, for the good of the people, not for the good of the dollar, not for the good of what this is going to be for my bottom line, but for the good of the people. And one of the prerequisites of going to medical school there for free, is that you have to come back to the US and work in very poor neighborhoods. So you can't get a free medical education and then come and practice for Wall Street bankers. No, you have to come back and practice for low-income people who don't have the kind of medical care that they really need to have good lives.

And so they took the compassion and love for people that they learned in Cuba, to the people in Haiti. And in fact, the first people that were there after the earthquake were the Cubans bringing their medical teams, bringing the medical disaster teams to Cuba to help. In fact, Cuba offered to send doctors to New Orleans after Katrina[5] to help the people there. But of course, the President and the U.S. administration refused.

TC: Okay, so continue telling me about what they said in terms of their experiences there.

---

5 Hurricane Katrina was a devastating Category 5 Atlantic hurricane that caused widespread damage and fatalities in the New Orleans area in late August 2005.

NIM: They shared their experiences, that it was their first opportunity to really put what they had learned to use; that the Haitian people are not just people waiting for a handout. That while they needed medical attention, they were able and willing, "Now what can we do to help our own people? How can we help ourselves? What can you teach us? What can you leave us with so that we're not a dependent people? But that we are a very resilient people, and we can do some things for ourselves." And so they loved the experience. They had an all-women's medical team that was there. I mean, they were so thrilled about that, and they plan to go back again.

TC: Well, that's a very wonderful and beautiful and inspiring story. So Rev. Lucius Walker, Pastors for Peace; sisters, brothers, anybody who wants a free medical education, and will serve the people with that education, get in touch with them, and that's how they can do that. That's wonderful. Okay, now, that is so wonderful. So tell me, going back to the first trip to Cuba, where you met Assata Shakur, can you tell us about that story and the story behind the story?

NIM: Okay, so when I knew that I was going to Cuba of course when I thought about Cuba, I thought about Assata Shakur. I mean, she's legendary. She's an exile there, and people had not heard anything from her in years. So I'm thinking, "Okay, well, you know, maybe she might speak to me," but yeah, of course, who am I? I'm this this little writer for *The Final Call* newspaper. I was there with reporters and writers from *Essence* magazine, *USA Today*, big name newspapers all across the country. I'm just little ole me. But as soon as I started, got there, you know, I started asking, of course, I'm Muslim, you know, where's the mosque? Cuba is known for being a non-religious country, even though there are a lot of Catholics there. People were saying, oh, there's a mosque and we'll try to show you where the mosque is. And so I was asking around and telling people that I spoke to I'm with *The Final Call*, and I would like to interview Assata Shakur, if I can. So the week went by, so by Friday, I said, "Okay well this is a lost cause. I'm not going to be able to connect with her."

But then that Friday evening, I got a call. And the person said, you know, "Did you find the mosque?" So I started thinking "Well, now, who has just asked me if I found the mosque?" and I said, "No, I didn't find the mosque, you know, but I am still looking" and she said, "Well, are you still interested in interviewing Assata Shakur?" and I was like, "Yeah." She said, "Well, here I am." And I'm like, I dropped the phone. I'm like, "Oh, my God, it's really her!" So I was like, "Okay, yes. I would love to interview you!" And then she said, "Okay, meet me across the street at the hotel at 2 pm." So I was like, "Well, what's the name of the hotel?" She said, "you'll find it meet me there at 2 pm. So I'm like, "Oh my God, all this undercover stuff." So I called DeWayne Wickham and said, "Oh my god, I have an interview with Assata Shakur, I can't go with you all to the beach tomorrow, I have to stay here to interview her!" And he was like, "Do whatever you have to do."

They left a photographer with me to go there and meet with her. So I could hardly sleep. So I was thinking about my questions, what I would ask her, I started doing more research, I was like "Why me? I mean, all these other big name people were here, you know why, you know, would she pick me?" So when we got there the first thing was no pictures, you know, because she said that she didn't want the pictures to get into the wrong hands and people be able to track where she was, all of that. So I understood that. Then I just kind of said, you know, "Why me?" You know, not that I mind. You know, "it's okay that you chose me," but just so for my own personal edification. And she said, "Because I trust *The Final Call* to tell my story." And I was, of course floored, and that, of course, gave a bigger responsibility for me to be able to tell her story.

And so that's kind of the "behind the story" of how I got it. It was a wonderful experience. We talked for like two hours. And I asked her questions about everything, you know? What she enjoyed about Cuba, etc. The one thing that we didn't go into was how she got to Cuba. She didn't want to go into those details. And I was happy because I didn't want somebody interviewing me, "Now how did she get there?! You tell us what you know!" "I know nothing! I'm only a reporter! I know nothing to put me in jail. I know nothing! I know nothing!" So she's just a wonderful, wonderful Black woman who just wanted a better life for herself, who was wrongfully accused, wrongfully convicted, and just felt like "I just can't live here in this jail, I have to do something better for myself." One of the things that really stuck out when I asked her what did she miss about being in America? And she said she missed Black culture. She loved being in Cuba, she loves the

Cuban culture, the people, but there's just a certain way about being a Black woman in America, I mean, she said our laughter. You know, the way we care for our children, the way we are, our music, the way we walk ...

TC: The way we only worth $5?[6]

NIM: Come on all of that!

[Laughter]

TC: In spite of all of that there's something that we still have, regardless of what the economists may say about our financial situation.

NIM: We can make a dollar out of 15 cents! That's what it means to be a Black woman! We take lemons and make lemonade every day! And so, you know, she missed those things. And you know, she missed seeing her daughter grow up. And so it was really a great interview. And the article is available online[7] if people want to read it, Nisa Islam Muhammad and Assata Shakur, and it was just a wonderful, wonderful experience. But it really gave me a very heavy burden of being responsible with her story. You know, as a reporter, and when we're telling someone else's story, it's a great responsibility to either accurately tell that story and not let American sensitivities and the American filter impede our ability to tell the actual story. And so I felt good about the story. People have seen it, the story went all over the world because it was the latest story from her in terms of her experiences in Cuba, and what was going on. And I felt really fortunate that I was able to do that.

TC: That is wonderful. Do you have any future plans to return to Cuba?

NIM: Anytime I can go to Cuba, I would love to go to Cuba. The thing that's really interesting about Cuba, I contrasted my trip to Cuba with my experience in Paris. So when I went to Paris in 2007, right during the height of the Iraq War. And, you know, talking to people there and you know "you damn Americans!" What? "The Iraq war, you got us into the Iraq War!" What? No, no, no, no, no, "*I* did not get us into anything. I didn't even vote for George Bush. I am not responsible!" But what the Europeans in Paris saw was that I was American, and I was responsible for an unwanted unnecessary war.

6 "Study Finds Median Wealth For Single Black Women at $5". *The Atlantic*, March 11, 2010
7 "Assata Shakur: From exile with love," FinalCall.com, June 11, 2002.

Very different experience in Cuba. In Cuba, they were able to differentiate Black people from the American administration, so that when I was talking to them about being an American, they were like, "Oh, we love you. You're Black. We understand your oppression. We understand the racism that you've experienced," and they did not blame me for the embargo that America has had and I was like, "Hallelujah! because I had nothing to do with any of this. Do not blame me!" But I'm just born in America. So very different, very different ways of looking at the same situation.

TC: And how long have you been a journalist?

NIM: I think I was born to be a journalist. But actually writing, I wrote in college. I graduated from the University of Maryland with a degree in psychology, unsure like a whole lot of young people, "What am I going to do with my life? What am I gonna do with a degree in psychology?" and then I realized in my senior year that I really wanted to write, that I enjoyed writing. Went to Howard University for a year, wrote for *The Hilltop*, Howard University's newspaper, and loved it, and began to write soon after that for *The Final Call* newspaper. Did that for a couple of years, left, did some more things then came back to the paper in the late 1990s, and have been writing for the paper ever since.

TC: How long have you been Muslim?

NIM: I have been Muslim 30 years, the majority of my adult life.

TC: So were you Muslim when you were writing for *The Hilltop* at Howard?

NIM: No, I think I had just started considering Islam, but I had not become a Muslim then. And so I was writing for the purposes of regular student life, and I loved writing the stories and telling people, I'm a storyteller. I love telling stories.

TC: Well, I understand what you're saying about probably being born to be a journalist, because I think it's becoming clearer to me now that that's what I was supposed to be doing. You know, media has always been around me. And my respect of media, my understanding of its power and my awe for media has always been there. But one thing I didn't do, I don't call myself a journalist, because I was conditioned by society to believe that a journalist is objective. And I'm like, "No, I'm not objective, you know, my people are oppressed." So I have a particular viewpoint and I take a particular side, a side that I don't always see represented, so I was like, "Okay, I'm not a journalist then." But I was a journalist. And it took, I'm grateful to KPFK for giving me the opportunity to actually get some training and do news. And I'm like "Wait a minute, I am a journalist. Back off, I'm claiming this term."

NIM: I think the thing is that objectivity is for everybody but "them," you know? They want everybody else to be objective. But if you look at the news, if you look at the news and how we got to the Iraq War,[8] there was no objectivity in that at all. You know, the objective people say, "Wait a minute, there aren't any weapons of mass destruction over there." But the main media, the propaganda machines that were out there, have to come back and apologize to the American people by saying "We fell for the hype."

TC: After how many died?

NIM: After so many people died. We fell for the hype. There were no weapons of mass destruction there and we got all these people in a war, all these people have died, maimed, injured, lives ruined because of a war because of a lie?

TC: France mad at us

NIM: France mad at us! I'm serious! Getting mad at me in Paris!

TC: Getting mad at little ole you!

NIM: Come on, makes no sense! But all because of a lie. All because of some supposed objectivity that was never objective from the beginning.

TC: So all of that to segue into … what have been some of your high points? What have been some of your low points?

NIM: You know, I love telling the stories that most people ignore, I love going into the little neighborhoods, Black communities, and telling the stories. I won an award from New America Media for best local reporting for a story I wrote about the DC police who had set up stop points for residents in a high crime area. So in order to go into the area, you had to

---

8 The Iraq War, also known as the Second Gulf War or Operation Iraqi Freedom, was a conflict that took place from 2003 to 2011. It was initiated by the United States-led coalition, with the primary objective of removing Saddam Hussein, the president of Iraq at the time, from power. The main reasons cited by the United States for launching the war were the alleged possession of weapons of mass destruction (WMDs) by Iraq and the perceived threat posed by the regime to regional stability and global security. However, subsequent investigations found no evidence of WMDs in Iraq.

stop at this police checkpoint, kind of like, apartheid or something. These little police checkpoints, say who you are, show identification before you can enter into this community. Now, supposedly, it was to reduce crime. But it also stifled the community members' ability to move in and out of the community. I went to the community and tried to do it myself, to experience what it was like for these community members to be there and be under these checkpoints. And so I won an award for that story.

I like telling the stories of our young people, of children and what's going on in their lives, and how they struggle to even get an interest to graduate from high school. I did a story on the low graduation rates for Latino youth. See we think we've got it bad, as Americans, and we were born here? Imagine coming here from another country and your parents don't speak the language and trying to struggle with high school and you have to go with your mom to clean up office buildings at night, from 12 to five, then go to sleep for a few hours and then go to high school. It's a rough story

TC: That sounds real rough.

NIM: It's a rough story. And people wonder why you fall asleep in class, and they wonder why you're doing poorly. And they don't understand that you can't go home and ask your parents for help with your homework because they don't speak the language. That you don't have anybody in your family that's ever gone to college. Well, that's true for a lot of Black people, too but at least we speak the language. And so these are some of the untold stories of the difficulties that people have that I like to tell.

TC: So are there any low points?

NIM: A low point? It's always a low point.

TC: Why is it always a low point?

NIM: I think part of the reason it's always a low point is because we don't have the resources and the budgets that other major newspapers have. And we're making a dollar out of 15 cents, we're always scrambling, we're always calling. We're always exchanging equipment with somebody, "Okay, I'm done with this camera but it's still got life in here, you can use it, you know, I saved up enough money to get a new digital or I saved up enough money to get a new recorder so you use this one," you know? So we're always trading.

... One of the things now I also write for a blog about Michelle Obama, the Michelle Obama Watch Blog, and it's an incredible experience. I'm the Washington correspondent and so I get to go to the White House, anything and everything about Michelle Obama. But it's interesting how she can do no right for some people. Now some people she can do no wrong, but other people she can do no right. She's in the garden planting with children and people are criticizing her because of what she has on. "Oh, she was all made up to go out and garden." Well, she's going out, you're going to always see her made up. How do you want her to look? You want her to look like a hag? What, how do you think, she is the First Lady? You want her to look like what? Like she just woke up? No, come on. That means just anything, she can do no right. She can do no right. But so I really love doing that. So that my only low point is that I think if there were more resources that it would be better.

TC: Anything else that I should know?

NIM: I think you should know that I say this to all writers: It's an incredible responsibility to tell stories. And that when you're telling people's stories, they are giving you their lives to tell and we either can show the good or bad of it, but sometimes we do both. But we also have to be able to inspire and give people hope. And that's what I try to do with all of my stories is give people hope because without hope we're just helpless. And too many of us feel helpless without a rope to hold on to and say you know what, there's some hope out there.

TC: Sister Nisa Islam Muhammad of *The Final Call* newspaper, thank you so much for your time.

NIM: Thank you! My pleasure!

Integrity Matters: Interview with Black Lives Matter Co-Founder Patrisse Cullors

Patrisse Cullors is an artist, abolitionist, and writer. A co-founder of Black Lives Matter, she is the author of the memoir When They Call You a Terrrorist *and* The Abolitionist's Handbook. *She believes in using "intergenerational healing work that centers love and collective care" as a means "to grow towards abolition." The following interview appeared on* Daily Kos *on November 27, 2015.*

• • •

In October 2015, *Cosmopolitan* magazine interviewed the founders of Black Lives Matter: Patrisse Cullors, Alicia Garza and Opal Tometi. The photo shoot and article were part of the magazine's "Fun Fearless 50, celebrating the world's most inspiring women." At the beginning of November, Cullors posted a Facebook status update where she was self-critical of participating in the shoot. The post stated:

Patrisse Marie Cullors-Brignac
November 7 at 9:50 pm

Last month Cosmopolitan *featured the BLM co-founders. We were styled by the Banana Republic. Someone I grew up with who is doing amazing activism pointed out that the clothes we were wearing was highly problematic. As someone who believes in international solidarity, with third world peoples. I want to take public accountability for not questioning the folks who dressed us in our shoot. I refuse to be a part of that trajectory. I'm learning, and I really appreciate my homegirl for calling me out the way she did."*

I decided to ask her about the issues raised in her self-criticism and a few other issues.

Thandisizwe Chimurenga: What was it that your friend, the one who criticized you, said to you?

Patrisse Cullors: "When you and your partners were featured in *Cosmopolitan*, you were wearing 'fast' clothing (like fast food) from brands like Zara, Banana Republic. Do you know these clothes are made in the global south? I covered stories on this where thousands of people have died making clothes for the West. Since you are a leader, I want to point this out to you, so you can tell your community not to endorse these products. We need to take a stand. Where do these cheap clothes come from? Who makes them? Why don't we see their faces?" She also sent me a link to a skit done by John Oliver.[1]

She also said, "But with the level of power you have, you can raise awareness, open eyes to the injustices young female garment workers face. They get abused, can barely eat, earn less than a dollar a day to make clothes for the West to wear for cheap ... there needs to be a more sustainable way of handling it."

TC: What is it about what she told you that made you feel you needed to speak publicly via social media about it?

PC: I was trained to believe in an international fight against U.S. imperialism. Labor rights are a key fight in the fight against global capitalism. I took my friend's critique seriously because my politics were being questioned and my ethics were being questioned. Why would I allow *Cosmopolitan* to dictate my politics and my ethics? I wouldn't, so when I received the critique it felt necessary to name it publicly so folks could see how we should be accountable to our ethics.

TC: You mentioned pressure to mainstream BLM – can you speak candidly on that?

---

1 John Oliver (1977-) is a British-American television host. Since 2014, Oliver has been the host of the HBO series *Last Week Tonight with John Oliver*.

PC: I think the biggest thing around mainstreaming BLM ... there's a seduction of mainstreaming BLM which could ultimately lead to diluting the message of BLM, and the message is about all Black lives mattering in this kind of moment in history, in the past, present and the future, and it's not just about the extra-judicial killings of Black people but a larger conversation and interrogation of anti-Black racism.

What can often happen is when anything becomes popular it can lose its weight, it can lose its politics, so I think it's important given this *Cosmopolitan* shoot and as someone who I really care about this person's politics, to call us out in particular and say you know, "that's pretty contradictory in what you all are calling for." I thought it was an important intervention.

TC: How do you plan on guarding against (Banana-republic-type mistakes) in the future?

PC: (Laughs). I think in the future, if I were to do that *Cosmopolitan* shoot again I would have had a serious conversation with *Cosmopolitan* about who's dressing us, what does this mean, how is this out of – or in alignment with – BLM. I think we said yes to it because we were excited and we were like "That's great! Visibility in this particular way is important," but I think it would be like having longer conversations and interrogating the mainstream spaces that we take up, who asks us to come in.

TC: How do you plan to protect BLM from going mainstream?

PC: I don't know if I can protect it. I think what I can do is stay true to what I believe is true for Black lives. Keep up that narrative, keep up that practice, and don't fall short around it.

TC: You obviously felt that the public needed to know this about you and BLM. What else do you feel the public needs to know that is pressing and does not seem to be getting out there?

PC: That's a good question. I don't know. I think I really value public accountability and so that's why I decided to be upfront about it.

TC: You touched on this a little, so I'd like to go back: what did you hope to accomplish with the *Cosmopolitan* shoot?

PC: The shoot was about entering spaces and places that wouldn't necessarily know the three co-founders of Black Lives Matter. I think there's a way folks on the Left can preach to the choir and not actually get people to join the team, and I think that the goal of the shoot was to expand our audience.

TC: Do you want to address any of the financial rumors surrounding BLM, i.e. *Politico*?[2]

PC: We weren't invited to that Democracy Alliance[3] meeting so I can't really speak on behalf of that. We're not going to the meeting and we weren't invited to it.

TC: A lot of people are utilizing social media and right wing websites to say that you all are "getting paid, bout to get paid, got paid," etc.

PC: The network has received funding from different foundations; as we are developing our infrastructure, we are working on hiring staff and we are working on figuring out the best ways to fund our local chapters. And part of that looks like not having just myself and Alicia and Opal figure that out but really work with our network to figure that out.

TC: How had the network been funded before you formally organized as a network?

PC: We didn't have money.

TC: There's what people are calling Black Lives Matter, the overall broad movement with everybody from DeRay McKesson to whomsoever, and then there's Black Lives Matter the network which has 26 chapters. Is the network formally incorporated as a non-profit?

PC: The network has a fiscal sponsor.

TC: And everybody else out there is just everybody else?

PC: Exactly. Everybody else has their own ... DeRay is working with Campaign Zero, we have different people working inside the movement eco-system.

TC: This recent Google grant,[4] was that money awarded to the Ella Baker Center[5] or to you?

---

2 "Major donors consider funding Black Lives Matter," *Politico*, November 13, 2015.
3 The Democracy Alliance is a network of progressive donors who coordinate their political donations to groups that the Alliance has endorsed. It has been described by *Politico* as "the country's most powerful liberal donor club". Members are required to contribute at least $200,000 a year.
4 "Google Pours Money Into The Fight Against Racial Injustice." *Huffington Post*, November 4, 2015
5 The Ella Baker Center organizes with Black, Brown, and low-income people to advance people-powered

PC: Ella Baker Center.

TC: What is the Ella Baker Center's relationship with Black Lives Matter?

PC: They have an employee that is one of the co-founders. They are part of the larger movement for Black lives.

TC: Had you been using your personal paycheck to fund Black Lives Matter?

PC: To be honest with you, this is my first year ever getting a salary as an organizer and having health insurance.

TC: Through the Ella Baker Center?

PC: Yes.

TC: Not even through Dignity and Power Now [which you founded]?

PC: No.

TC: Anything else that needs to be known?

PC: I got love for the people, and the non-profit industrial complex is not the way we're going to win.

TC: But you're going to utilize it for this time period anyway?

PC: Yes. The non-profit industrial complex is not going to get us free, and the biggest thing is how do we insure that in our non-profits, we're actually fighting for Black lives? That looks like hiring Black people, building out Black projects, and not being afraid to use the word "Black."

TC: Does Black Lives Matter have any plans on building anything in Ferguson, MO? The network?

PC: We are in connection with lots of groups in Ferguson. The group that we helped support the most was the Organization for Black Struggle (OBS), who we helped get a budget. They didn't have a budget before the uprising. We see OBS as part of our network.

TC: We hear about how Black Lives Matter grew and flourished after the murder of Mike Brown in Ferguson, Missouri.[6] We also hear about how Black Lives Matter basically was started after the acquittal of George

---

campaigns for racial and economic justice. ellabakercenter.org

6 See note on page 61

Zimmerman for the murder of Trayvon Martin.[7] Does BLM have any projects planned for [Florida]?

PC: Not the network, we don't have any chapters there but we do have groups that we feel are our strong strategic partners like Dream Defenders[8] who are doing amazing work.

I think the other thing that's important is that the network is trying to be this thing that brings an alternative platform for a Black Left. An alternative platform for Black people of all generations to show up to this current moment, and that can look like building a chapter, or having your own organization and being affiliated to the network, but it's really about trying to get us stronger as a Black Left.

TC: A lot of people are critical of BLM, the movement the network all of it, because they say that you don't really come out and protest when Black people kill other Black people. I understand the concept of state violence – how not just police violence but the conditions of life that Black people are forced to live under are violent, and I understand that ultimately that is the source of intra-racial or Black on Black violence. Is that BLM's position?

PC: Yes, and also it's two-fold. One is that Black people have been fighting against the harm in our communities forever. They're dismissed. There's been lots of folks historically who have showed up for Black people. Most of our movement projects are about trying to mitigate the harm we cause to one another and I think that's really important [to know]. If you think about the Black Panther Party – they were gang members before they became the Panther Party. If you think about so many different truces that happened in the [Los Angeles] Black community after the 1992 uprising and the cops broke that truce up. So there's a way in which this conversation needs to start with 'we have been fighting against the harm in our community.'

TC: Yes Black people have always done that, but part of this criticism if not the majority of it is directed at you and BLM the network/movement.

---

7 Trayvon Martin (1995-2012) was a 17-year-old African-American fatally shot in Sanford, Florida, by George Zimmerman. The police said there was no evidence to refute his claim of self-defense, and Florida's stand-your-ground law prohibited them from arresting or charging him. After national media focused on the incident, Zimmerman was eventually charged and tried, but a jury acquitted him of second-degree murder and manslaughter in July 2013.

8 dreamdefenders.org

PC: What I'm saying is that BLM in and of itself the network the project the process the movement is about mitigating harm in our communities

TC: Understanding everything that I've said and you said, when BLM raises up as a crucial plank the visibility of Black trans and Black queer people, Black trans people in particular because of the violence they have suffered, a lot of that violence is intra-racial. In other words, there's a plank there for Black trans people, but not a plank for Black people in general around intra racial violence.

PC: Yeah I hear that. I think in this context though, when we're talking about trans folks, specifically, there's never been a conversation about Black trans people and that the reality is when people are talking about Black on Black violence they're not actually talking about Black trans people, they're talking about Black men, 'Cis' Black men.[9] Black on Black violence is [usually] 'Cis' against 'Cis' and the reason why we're uplifting Black trans women in this conversation is because up until now, the only time Black on Black violence was acceptable was to kill Black trans women, and so we have to uplift [them].

---

9 Cis = Cisgender, i.e. having a gender identity which matches the sex one was assigned at birth

"Who Do You Call When the Police Are the Problem?" – Ramona Africa

Speaking at Faith United Methodist Church in Los Angeles, CA, April 17, 2004. Transcribed by Paul Goettlich from the video by Ralph Cole of JusticeVision Democracy University volume 60.1 The moderator for this event was Sister Thandisizwe Chimurenga, co-host of Some of Us Are Brave *on KPFK 90.7 FM.*

• • •

Thandisizwe Chimurenga: I attended a lecture a couple of weeks ago. And people came to see this particular speaker. The people who were with him said, "Well, you all know who this person is. That's why you're here. So here he is." I thought that was an interesting introduction.

You all know who Ramona Africa is. You all have some semblance of an idea. That's why you're here tonight. But I still believe in giving credit and recognition where it is due.

I've been with Sister Ramona for a couple of days now, and I find it hard to introduce her without almost giving her lecture. I don't want to do that. But I do want to, as I said, give credit where credit is due. And I do want to tell you something about this Sister.

Ramona Africa is the Minister of Communication for the MOVE organization. And I would like to say that Ramona Africa grew up attending Catholic schools in Philadelphia. She graduated from Temple University. And she was set to go into law school when she encountered the injustice and oppression that was meted out towards the MOVE organization.

Subsequently [she was] introduced to the teachings of John Africa[1] and it changed her life.

Ramona Africa is a survivor of the 1985 massacre of the MOVE organization in Philadelphia, Pennsylvania, where C-4, a military explosive, was dropped on the home of her and her family. Six adults and five children were subsequently murdered in that massacre. Ramona is the only adult to survive. One child survived with her.

The city block was destroyed. Sixty-one Black folks' homes were destroyed by the fire caused by the military explosive dropped by the city of Philadelphia in conjunction with the state of Pennsylvania, and the federal government of the United States of America.

No one has served a day in jail because of that crime against humanity. Sister Ramona, however, because she survived, was convicted of survival and spent seven years in prison. She was sentenced to a minimum of 16 months or a maximum of seven years. After the 16 months they told her, "We will let you go if you leave the MOVE organization." She told them where they could go. And she did her entire seven-year sentence.

She was released in 1992. She hit the ground running. She has not stopped yet.

The Jericho Amnesty Coalition Los Angeles exists to raise awareness of the existence of political prisoners, prisoners of war and exiles, to agitate for their release and for amnesty. It is in this vein that we have brought Sister Ramona Africa here to Los Angeles so that she will tell you about her story and the story of her family, about the MOVE 9 who have been in prison since 1978, about Mumia Abu-Jamal's[2] case and the newest developments.

---

1 John Africa (1931-1985) was the founder of MOVE, a Philadelphia-based, predominantly Black organization active from the early 1970s. He and his followers were killed in a residence which served as the headquarters of MOVE, in a fire after the Philadelphia Police Department bombed the house with C4-explosive, and deliberately let the fire rage until it was out of control following a standoff and firefight between MOVE and police.

2 Mumia Abu-Jamal (born 1954) is an American political activist and journalist who was convicted of murder and sentenced to death in 1982 for the 1981 murder of a Philadelphia police officer. After numerous appeals, his death penalty sentence was overturned by a federal court. In 2012, he joined the general prison population. During his imprisonment, Abu-Jamal has published books and commentaries on social and political issues; his first book was *Live from Death Row* (1995).

Mumia Abu-Jamal, an award-winning, brilliant writer, commentator on KPFK, a brilliant journalist who is on death row as we speak, was sentenced to death wrongly in 1981 for the murder of a Philadelphia policeman. His sentence of death was overturned yet he remains locked on death row. April 24 will be Mumia Abu-Jamal's 50th birthday. It will be his 23rd birthday behind prison walls.

This is why we have brought Sister Ramona Africa here. Just to remind you... I know you all know who she is, but as we said, we must give credit where credit is due.

Ladies and gentlemen, brothers and sisters, friends and allies, Sister Ramona Africa.

[Audience applauds wildly]

Ramona Africa: Thank you. Thank you. Thank you very much.

I appreciate the warm welcome. It does my heart good. Thank you very much.

And I want to thank Sister Thandi. I want to thank everybody involved in bringing me here to the West Coast and making this program happen. I want people to know that Thandi has worked tirelessly arranging programs for me to speak at. And she too deserves credit where credit is due.

OK. I generally start a lecture with a quote from John Africa. And I am going to do that. But one thing I want to say before I get into that, just very simply, because we are in a church. And that is John Africa pointed out something to MOVE years ago. And I never forgot it because, as Sister Thandi told you, I went to Catholic school for 12 years, first to 12th grade. I was raised Catholic.

One thing that stuck with me when John Africa told it to me, because of my background, was that if you want to know the mentality of government, look at one thing. Go back to the Bible and look at how when the word spread that the Christ child was going to be born, this bringer of truth and peace. What did the government do? What did King Herod do?

According to the Bible, he sent out his soldiers to kill every newborn male child because he wasn't about to have truth and peace upsetting his applecart.

The point is that the mentality of government has not changed in 2000 and four years. Because government, on whatever level, is still threatened by truth...by the principle of peace. It is not in their interest. It is not what government is about. And governments have existed to stifle and stamp out truth. So, I just had to point that out because I just remembered so clear when that example was given to me by John Africa.

Now, let me start with a quote from John Africa. This particular quote is very, very important. And anybody who claims to be a revolutionary will see it as important because it's fundamental and it's something that we must all understand.

To quote John Africa, the coordinator:

> *You can be wrong and still be legal. But when you say you're right and do wrong, you ain't right no more. Ain't no such thing as a legal right because right ain't legal. It's natural. If being legal was the same as being right you wouldn't have legal problems. You got a legal system and your legal system is filled with problems. But if the system was right, it would be just that – right.*
>
> *When you officials demand people are to follow your procedures to defend themselves, you are demanding that people give up their own procedure. MOVE's against the system. We've made it clear that we're against the system. We ain't benefiting nothing when we do things as the system instead of as MOVE.*
>
> *Your way is to stop us. Our way is to stop you. So, how can we benefit by you...by doing things as you? It ain't just a question of MOVE against the court. It is an issue of MOVE against the system. And it ain't procedure to help what you're against. And you officials know it. We're against the system. You want to stop us. And to ask us to go along with your procedure is to help you stop us. Volunteer our freedom to be imprisoned. Put handcuffs on our wrists and will lock our own selves up. How else can it be? You ain't for us. You're against us.* – John Africa

I want to be certain that people understand exactly what's being said here. What John Africa is telling people is that you cannot look to your oppressor, to your enemy, for the diagram, for the tactic, for the way to stop them from oppressing you.

Could Jews look to Hitler for the means to stop the Holocaust? Could Black South Africans look to members of the apartheid regime for the way to end apartheid? Could African slaves brought to this country look to the slave owners for the means to end slavery?

Of course not.

Well, what we have got to understand in the year 2004, for those who don't understand it, is that we cannot look to this system that is oppressing and exploiting and enslaving, not only people but all life, for the means to stop that. Why would they give you the way to destruct them... to destroy them...to end their reign? They're not going to do it.

They have created this concept called *legal* to trick people... to give you the impression that, of course, resistance is accepted. "Of course, protest is accepted. Of course you can challenge anything that you don't agree with. But you have to do it within our framework. We have created these little procedures based on this concept called legal. And any gripes that you have, you're free to air them. But you have to do it this way."

Well, thanks to John Africa, MOVE is not imprisoned by that concept called *legal*. It was invented by the oppressor. They are the orchestrator, the script writer of legality. They change it day to day, week to week, month to month. It's one thing one day and something else another day.

That's their reference not ours.

If *legal* was synonymous with right, then explain how slavery could be legal...apartheid...the Holocaust.

Right now, you have a U.S. Supreme Court that wants you to accept their legal ruling that it's OK to execute an innocent person – that as long as a person had a "fair trial," as long as they have exhausted their appeals, if they are this close [Ramona holds up her hand with her thumb and index finger nearly touching] to being executed, and someone comes forward and confesses, gives details, and in all likelihood – we can't say positively, but it could be the person who committed the murder – and the person on death row, their lawyer goes running into the courts saying, "Hey look, we got new evidence. You got to stop this. You got to at least have a hearing and check this evidence out."

That's what happened with this case called the Herrera case — a Spanish brother in Texas, the home of George Bush. The U.S. Supreme Court looked at his lawyer like he was crazy. And they told him very clearly, "We don't have to do anything. At this point, innocence is not the issue."

Now, if innocence is not the issue, then what IS the issue?

They proceeded to *execute* that man. And then they did it again and another case based on that Herrera ruling.

It was all legal.

But was it right?

Are we supposed to accept it because they put a label of *legal* on it?

No.

This is what John Africa had taught MOVE from the very beginning of MOVE— not to be imprisoned by the training of this system. Because these people are no joke. They *train* you how to think. They train people to start from their reference. "Don't look beyond that. Start here. And don't go any further."

Well, John Africa took us outside of that box. And we look at things differently than this system. And nobody is going to convince us to accept enslavement, exploitation, [and] insanity because somebody puts the word *legal* on it, particularly our enemy.

This is the reality... the mentality of MOVE people. So, when you wonder why this system comes down on MOVE the way it did and still does, it is that kind of thinking. They don't want us influencing others to start thinking like that.

I'm going to read something to and then maybe you can tell me what this is about.

> *All experience has shown that mankind are more disposed to suffer while evils are sufferable than to right themselves by abolishing the forms to which they are accustomed. But when a long train of abuses reduced them under absolute despotism, it is their right, it is their duty to throw off such government and to provide new guards for their future security.*

Now, MOVE didn't write that.

The Panthers didn't write that.

The SLA, the BLA didn't write that.

The Young Lords didn't write that.

[Someone in audience asks, "Who wrote that?"]

That is the Declaration of Independence.

And what it's telling you is that this country was supposed to be founded, according to them, on the principle that you when you are reduced under despotism... under oppression by the government, that it is not only your right, but it is your *duty*, your *obligation* to fight back... to make things right, even if it means *abolishing* that government.

[Great applause and shouts from audience]

The question then becomes, how can MOVE members, Panthers, Mumia, Leonard Peltier,[3] Puerto Rican Independentistas, and a host of others be labeled terrorists... criminal for applying the Declaration of Independence?

You see, you can't have it both ways.

Either resistance and defying of legality in favor of justice and what is right is to be applauded and awarded and encouraged and celebrated, like they do every Fourth of July, *or* it's to be penalized and punished and crushed.

But you can't have it both ways.

If you're going to tell me today that the defying legality and going to war with government is completely unacceptable, then wipe the Fourth of July off the map. It doesn't exist anymore.

And if you're saying that it is to be celebrated with fireworks and celebration, then why are all these people in prison for doing just that?

How *is* it that a Nathan Hale,[4] a Patrick Henry,[5] a Paul Revere[6] are

---

3 Leonard Peltier (born 1944) is a Native American activist and a member of the American Indian Movement (AIM) who, following a controversial trial, was convicted of two counts of first-degree murder in the deaths of two FBI agents in a 1975 shooting on the Pine Ridge Indian Reservation in South Dakota. He was sentenced to two consecutive terms of life imprisonment and has been imprisoned since 1977.

4 Nathan Hale (1755-1776) was an American soldier and spy during the Revolutionary War. In 1776 he volunteered to go behind enemy lines and gather information, but was captured by the British. Hale was hanged in a public execution in New York City. His death made him a symbol of American patriotism.

5 Patrick Henry (1736-1799) was an American attorney and orator. Henry is remembered for his oratory and as an enthusiastic promoter of the fight for independence. He was a slaveholder throughout his adult life.

6 Paul Revere (1735-1818) was an American patriot and silversmith who played a significant role in the American

celebrated every year as freedom fighters, heroes? But a Delbert Africa,[7] a Geronimo Pratt,[8] a Mumia Abu-Jamal, a Dylcia Pagán,[9] a Marilyn Buck[10] are called urban terrorists?

How is that possible?

These are things we need to really start thinking about and confronting this system with when it confronts us with those labels of illegality and violence and what we don't have the right to do.

They put it out there. So throw it back in their face when they come at us.

This is what the MOVE organization has been doing for over 30 years now...close to 35 years.

The MOVE organization started out in the early 1970s as a family brought together by John Africa. You know, John Africa brought people together from all different walks of life – rich, poor, educated, uneducated, various races and nationalities, various religions that people were involved in. He brought us altogether and made us a family of revolutionaries.

He gave us one single principle to live by. And that is respect and reference for all life – for our Mama... Mama Nature.

And when you respect life and respect the source of life, you understand that the coordinator of life put *every* species of life here to live in freedom.

Slavery does not come from life... from God. That's an invention of man that is in *conflict* with life, with God. And it is *not* to be accepted.

So, the MOVE organization started out with demonstrations – peaceful

---

Revolution. He is best known for his famous "Midnight Ride" on April 18, 1775, during which he rode on horseback from Boston to Lexington to warn the colonial militia that British troops were approaching.

7 Delbert Africa (1946-2020) was one of nine members of MOVE that were imprisoned on third-degree murder charges following an August 1978 armed standoff with Philadelphia police. In January 2020, Africa was released after spending 42 years behind bars. He died that June. He always maintained his innocence.

8 Elmer "Geronimo" Pratt (1947-2011), was a decorated military veteran and a high-ranking member of the Black Panther Party. The FBI targeted Pratt in the early 1970s. Pratt was convicted in 1972 for a 1968 murder; he served 27 years in prison. He was freed in 1997 when his conviction was vacated due to the prosecution's having withheld exculpatory evidence that tended to prove his innocence.

9 Dylcia Noemi Pagán (1946-) was a Puerto Rican member of the FALN (a group which fought for Puerto Rican independence during the 1970s) who in 1981 received a sentence of 55 years for seditious conspiracy and other charges. She was released early after President Bill Clinton extended clemency in 1999.

10 Marilyn Buck (1947-2010) was imprisoned for her participation in the 1979 prison escape of Assata Shakur, the 1981 Brink's robbery and the 1983 U.S. Senate bombing. Buck received an 80-year sentence, which she served in federal prison, from where she published numerous articles and other texts. She was released on July 15, 2010, less than a month before her death at age 62 from cancer.

demonstrations at unsafe boarding homes for the elderly where they were being physically and emotionally abused, where their Social Security checks were all but stolen from them. We demonstrated at the zoo and the circus against the abuse and enslavement of animals. Because if you wonder where the enslavement of people comes from, it comes because people allowed another species of life to be enslaved. So when you make an allowance for enslavement, don't think it's going to just stop there.

[Audience applauds]

We did various, various peaceful demonstrations. We confronted representatives of DuPont Chemical, Dow Chemical about them poisoning the environment – putting poison in our air and our water and our soil, causing disease, causing people to be sick, causing life to be sick.

And these people try to trick folks by seemingly admitting that, "Yeah, there's a problem with pollution in the water from their factories. But you know we're taking care of that. Our scientists have invented a water filter that you can buy from us for $29.99. That'll take care of your water."

And MOVE is like, "You must be out of your mind. You're going to make billions of dollars poisoning the environment, poisoning our water, and then create some gadget that poisons the water making it, and then you're going to sell it to us? And that's supposed to be the solution to the problem you caused?"

No, we ain't going for that. And we made people look at that and think about it cannot be tricked by the system.

Initially, officials would send cops out to our demonstrations. They would just stand by. They would take pictures of us. They would record what we were saying. And just monitor us.

But as they saw that people were listening to us, that people were coming up to us and talking to us, asking questions and seeing things a little clearer about this system that we live under, they realized they had a problem.

So they did what they always do. You know the pattern of this system don't change. They came at us with the soft soap, you know, the velvet gloves. [Ramona motions as if putting on a glove] they wanted to give us funding so that we could set up an office and, you know, work within the system...that kind of thing.

We let them know straight up that "We don't want your money. We don't want your office. We don't want no position in this system. We don't want *anything* from you. All we want from you is to leave us alone."

So, when they realized that we meant it, that we could not be bought, that we could not be bribed or co-opted, then they came with the next step, which is always the iron fist... you know, the brutality. And when MOVE people would go out to set up a peaceful demonstration at some institution of this system, the cops would be there as usual. Only this time, they tell us, "You got to pack up and leave. You cannot demonstrate here. You got to go."

And we would look at them like, "What is wrong with you? What are you talking about? We got to go? We can't demonstrate? Isn't this America, we tell people you have freedom of speech, freedom to protest, freedom of association and assembly, the freedom to assemble together? What, does the Constitution say 'except MOVE'?"

Of course they didn't want to hear anything we had to say. And that's when the beating and brutality started. MOVE men would be beaten bloody, into unconsciousness and broken limbs by cops. The MOVE women were beaten by cops. Pregnant MOVE women were beaten, stomped, kicked by cops – beat, stomped, kicked into miscarriage. A three-week old baby was knocked to the ground along with his mother who was holding him and trampled to death. His head was crushed.

This is the insanity and brutality that this system came to MOVE with.

MOVE people decided that we needed to make some things clear to this system. We're nobody's whipping post. And we made it clear to this system that we believe in peace. We are a peaceful people. We are uncompromisingly opposed to violence. But we are not stupid. We are John Africa taught. And we understand very clearly the difference between violence and self-defense. We *do not* believe in violence. But we *do* believe in self-defense.

We made it clear that you are not violent when you defend yourself. But you *are* violent if you are attacked and *refuse* to defend yourself because then you are encouraging, perpetuating, and endorsing violence— the worst form of violence. Because then you are masochistic... suicidal. And MOVE is neither masochistic or suicidal. You slap my cheek and I ain't turning the other cheek. I'm going to stop slapping right there.

[Audience applauds]

And there is nothing violent about that. It's *stopping* the violence. Okay?

There is not one species of life that Mama have put on this earth that does not defend itself when attacked.

Who do these people think they are to try to convince you that, unlike any other species of life, you don't have the right to defend yourself?

"If there is a problem you come to us and we'll take care of it." [As if said by the police]

Well, excuse me. What happens when *you* be the problem? [As if responding to police]

[Audience applauds]

You see, August 8, 1978, and a video, a very good video that was done on the police attack on MOVE, there's footage of this older Black woman. She's being interviewed. And she's saying how she was upstairs on the second floor of her house and all of a sudden her front door busts open and all these people come running into her house because the cops were on horseback... and they're just riding around with their nightsticks beating people, attacking people. People were trying to get away from them and ran into her house. She said she was so upset [because] she saw people bruised and bloody and everything. She ran to her phone. She picked up the phone and... stopped and like..."Well, damn, who do I call? Who do I call?"

[Audience applauds and laughs]

The point is, if you do not defend yourself, how can you expect anybody else to do that for you? Self-defense is *the* law. The law of life, the law of God that *nobody* has the right to take from you.

This is what MOVE made clear to this system. Well, you know they wasn't having that. And they didn't want us influencing *anybody else* with that kind of thinking.

So they tried to manufacture a reason to exterminate the MOVE organization. And this is the best they could come up with in 1977-78. They said, "Well, MOVE, we hate to tell you this, but your home, the house that you all live in has housing code violations. There's no screens and these windows." And you know, a few other ridiculous things like that.

And we said, "Oh yeah. Right. Okay."

And they kept pushing it, that there were housing code violations in the house, and that we had to vacate the house because, you know, it wasn't safe.

Now, when did this government become concerned about poor folks, particularly Black folks living in a house that has housing code violations? Why did they become concerned with that?

[Audience applauds]

But this is what they used try to manufacture a reason to come at MOVE. An order was issued saying that we should vacate MOVE headquarters by August 1st of 1978.

Well, some MOVE people were coordinated to go on other activities in Richmond, VA and in Rochester, NY. And the government knew that some MOVE people went to other cities…went on to other activities. I mean, they had us under surveillance. They followed us.

Nevertheless, on August 1st a judge issued warrants not simply for the MOVE people that were still in MOVE headquarters, but for every MOVE member that he could possibly think of…any and every MOVE member that he knew, even though they knew that some of these people were not even in the house. So obviously, that was not the issue – the house. They just wanted an excuse to come in on us.

I guess they got their little plan of attack together. And on August 8, 1978, in the wee hours of the morning, hundreds of cops and firefighters came out to our home, armed for war with one intent, one mission – to exterminate every living being in that house.

In their frenzy to kill MOVE they ended up killing one of their own. And MOVE can prove it. We know it. And this government knows it. Because a police officer was shot.

He was shot in the back of the neck with a bullet traveling on a downward angle. He was standing on street level leaning against a telephone pole, facing MOVE headquarters. MOVE people, by the police's own admission, are in the basement of MOVE headquarters.

Even if you believe that MOVE people were shooting up out of that basement at cops, they would have to be doing just that – shooting up out of the basement.

Now, explain to me how you can shoot up and shoot somebody with the bullet travelling on a downward angle AND around in back of them when they are facing you?

Maybe the CIA and the FBI... the ATF got weapons that do all that kind of tricky stuff. But nobody out on the street has it.

But this is what they must be saying to say that MOVE people killed this cop.

After arresting my family and taking everybody into custody they sent bulldozers out and *completely* demolished MOVE headquarters....completely demolished MOVE headquarters. Understand, a murder had been committed. Somebody was dead. The house became the alleged scene of the crime. How do you destroy vital evidence like that? How you destroy the scene of the crime?

That you're telling me that these people believed that MOVE killed the cop and destroyed the evidence at the scene of the crime? Not gonna happen. They destroyed the evidence because they knew all it would show is how they shot thousands of bullets in on MOVE. That's why they destroyed it.

Nine of my family members were charged with murder. Not, one charged with murder of the cop shot with one bullet from one gun... *nine* people were charged with murder. Not one charged with murder and the other eight with conspiracy, all nine were charged with murder.

How do nine people fire one bullet? How is that possible?

All nine were tried and all nine were convicted of murder and sentenced to thirty-year minimums and 100 year maximum sentences.

A day or so after Judge Edward Malmed sentenced MOVE people to prison, Mumia Abu-Jamal heard Judge Malmed on a radio talk show in Philadelphia. So he called in. He said, "Judge Malmed I have one question. Who killed police officer James Grant?"

The judge responded, "I haven't the faintest idea."

That's what he said.

After just sentencing nine of my family members to 100 years each in prison, this man admitted that.

Now, you wonder why Mumia is sitting on death row? [It's] because of journalism just like that...exposing these people, asking the simple powerful question.

Our brother Mumia was the *only* journalist that covered MOVE consistently and accurately. He could not and would not be intimidated. He could not be bought off with a paycheck. He was not looking to be the next Morley Safer,[11] or Ed Bradley,[12] or Peter Jennings.[13] Mumia is truly the voice of the voiceless.

He got his start in journalism writing for the Black Panther Party newspaper. Mumia was not trying to climb up the corporate ladder. He simply wanted to tell the truth... put out information for people... much-needed information.

So, when you wonder why Mumia sits on death row, why they framed him up...well, because of who he is. Mumia is not on death row for the accusation of murder. Mumia is on death row because they cannot control him, or co-opt him, and because he exposes them.

[Audience applauds]

That's right. And we don't forget that. You know, we want that made clear to people because we don't burn our energy going back and forth with people, debating with people about this system's interpretation of innocence or guilt.

We *know* who's guilty. We *know* who's the criminal. We're not confused about that.

So we fight for our brother. And we don't let *nobody* get in our face telling us that Mumia's guilty and he should be executed.

Let me tell you something:

---

11 Morley Safer (1931-2016) was a broadcast journalist, reporter, and correspondent for CBS News. He was best known for his long tenure on the news magazine *60 Minutes*.
12 Ed Bradley (1941-2006) was a broadcast journalist and news anchor. He was best known for his reporting on *60 Minutes* and CBS News.
13 Peter Jennings (1938-2005) served as the sole anchor of *ABC World News Tonight* from 1983 until his death in 2005.

As the only adult to survive the May 13 bombing, nobody is going to tell me that anybody in this system is in prison for the accusation of murder. If murder was the issue, why aren't those people who bombed and murdered our babies in prison?

Why aren't *they* on death row next to Mumia?

You understand?

Nobody...nobody is going to convince us that this is acceptable and that their interest is justice.

Oh no! No, no, no, no, no.

So, MOVE continues to fight...

[Ramona takes a drink of water and clears her throat]

I've been talking for days and days...

[Audience laughs]

OK.

Nobody is going to convince us that this system...that their interest, their goal is justice.

No way!

This government dropped a *bomb*... on me and my family simply because we would not accept them keeping our innocent family members in prison.

They tried to tell *you* that the reason they came out to our home in May of 1985 was because some neighbors complained about MOVE.

Well, excuse me, I'm not saying that some neighbors may not have had a complaint about MOVE. Maybe they did. I'm sure they did.

But what neighborhood in this country exists where some neighbor doesn't have a complaint about some other neighbor?

[Someone in audience shouts out, "that's right"]

But the question is, when did this government start caring about Black folks complaining about their neighbors? When did that happen? When did the FBI, the CIA, state and local governments become involved in neighborhood disputes?

They want you to believe that a few Black people at 62nd and Osage had a complaint about their neighbors and got *that* kind of response?

If anybody tells you that... any official tries to get in your face and tell you that, you need to slap them for insulting your intelligence. You know?

[Audience applauds and shouts]

They came out to our home in May of 1985 to silence our right to protest the ongoing imprisonment of our MOVE sisters and brothers. We was turning the heat up on them...*exposing* them at every turn and they wanted an end to it.

In the words of Wilson Goode, a so-called Black man who was mayor at the time – he wanted a permanent end to MOVE – that's what he said.

And toward that end they waged a full-scale war against MOVE on May 12, 1985. That's when they converged out there and started setting up high-powered weaponry. Mother's Day, Sunday, May 12, 1985. And it went into Monday, May 13. But they came out there on Mother's Day.

What could MOVE have done to warrant them dropping a *bomb* on us? We wasn't selling drugs. We wasn't raping and robbing nobody. We weren't accused of murder or assaulting anybody.

What could they *possibly* use to justify such a thing?

Nothing.

They really didn't feel like they had to.

They felt like they could just say, "We got some complaints about MOVE."

And when people heard the word MOVE they'd go like, "Oh, well, you know, I can understand that."

That's what they thought. That's what they were banking on. That's what they *used* the media to paint a certain picture on MOVE that *they* hoped would cause people to *think* that way and *accept* what they did simply because it was MOVE.

Didn't work out that way. People far and wide around the world understood that something foul and dirty happened that day and that there was *no* justification for it... *no justification*.

And this system... even though they *think* they got away with it, because no official was *ever* legally held accountable for the events of that day...

You know, five babies and six adults were murdered alive...burned alive that day. They dropped a bomb on our home with no notice at all.

And then when the bomb ignited a fire and the fire department was *immediately* notified that there was a fire, they made a conscious decision that they weren't going to fight it...that they were going to let it burn.

What situation have you *ever* heard of where the fire department is right there ... a fire department that put tons of water on our house earlier when there was no fire, suddenly makes a decision that now that there *is* a fire, they're not going to put any water on it? They're going to let it burn?

When have firefighters *ever* stood by and decided to let a fire burn, knowing that there are men, women, babies, and animals inside the dwelling that's on fire?

[Someone in audience gives an answer]

Yeah... 1921 in Tulsa, Oklahoma. I understand that.

That is the only other time that that has happened where Black folks were bombed and murdered by the government....and the KKK...well, same thing. Ain't no difference.

[Ramona laughs and audience claps]

There is no difference.

But the point is, that's what they did. And when MOVE people, who are in the basement of our home realized that our home was on fire, we immediately tried to get our children and our animals out of that burning building...that blazing inferno, only to be met by a barrage of police gunfire deliberately aimed at us to make sure that nobody survived that attack.

At least twice I tried to come out of there and bring some people out of there... bring some children out of there and was shot back in... you know, forced back in.

At that point, you are in a position where you're either going to choke to death on the smoke and burn alive, or you try to get out and possibly be shot to death.

Well, I tried to get out one more time and I was able to get a little boy out of there. And you could hear the gunfire hitting all around us...whizzing all around us.

But we survived that because we got out and got just a little bit away from the house. And cops grabbed us...grabbed the little boy... threw me down on the ground... handcuffed me. And we were the only two to survive.

The point is: five babies and six adults were murdered.

I wasn't charged with their murder.

Somebody murdered them. They were not only burned alive, but they were found to have bullet fragments in them from when the cops shot at them.

What more do you need to be charged with murder?

They arrested me immediately, even though there was no evidence that I did anything but come out of the house. They *admitted* to shooting at least 10,000 rounds of bullets in that house by *their* own admission. They *admit* to letting the fire burn.

They *admit* to this stuff. The whole world saw them drop that bomb on our house.

And they get investigated.

I get arrested.

When you investigate something that means you don't know what happened and you're trying to piece together what happened.

But now, if you don't *know*, how did you know enough to arrest me?

How did you determine that I was wrong?

But they did. They arrested me.

And as Thandi told you, I was eventually convicted of riot and conspiracy. The charges merged into just the riot charge. And I was sentenced to 16 months to 7 years in prison.

They put that stipulation that Thandi told you, and several other sisters and brothers who became eligible for parole.

Not one of us accepted it...that we would leave MOVE...sever all ties with MOVE in order to get released.

Not one of us accepted it.

[Audience shouts and applause loudly]

And because of all our uncompromising stance, and us exposing them, and people far and wide putting pressure on them, it was the government... the parole board that had to *back up* and parole MOVE people without that stipulation.

MOVE didn't give no ground. *They* had to. *They* had to.

And as Thandi told you, I came home in 1992 and have been out here, you know, educating and informing people, hopefully motivating people not simply to free the MOVE 9 or Mumia, but to free yourself. You know?

Understand where freedom comes from.

Freedom is not in leaving one building called a prison for another building called your house, your home, or some other building. Freedom – true freedom – is in the *absence* of this system. THAT'S where true freedom lies.

And this is the work that the MOVE organization is doing. And it's the work that our brother Mumia recognized and supported and became a strong MOVE supporter. You know? Which is another reason why they want to get rid of Mumia...another reason.

Our brother is that the very *last* stages of his appeals.

Understand something.

When I told you about the Herrera case, they're doing a similar thing in Pennsylvania with Mumia.

There is a man named Arnold Beverly who came forward and stated... confessed that he was the one that killed policeman Daniel Faulkner. He gave details, described what he was wearing, where he was at. This information matched statements they had gotten from people back in 1981. It all clicked. It all jived.

So, when Mumia had evidentiary hearings in the state court, particularly a post-conviction appeal hearing in front of Judge Pamela Dembe, the court decided that, "Yeah, well, you know, there's this confession. But we don't believe it's credible. Nobody's gonna believe that. And furthermore, it's too late. It should have been filed by such and such time, and it's too late."

And MOVE's position is: It's not credible? You haven't even had a hearing on it. How did you determine that? Based on what?

Secondly, *too late*? We're not talking about a meaningless legal procedure here. We're talking about a man's life. He is still alive. He is still in the courts. He still sits on death row. How can it *possibly* be too late? We're not accepting that.

People should be *outraged* that this government would just throw words out there like that and expect you to *accept it*.

MOVE don't accept it.

And we have... I have been going all over telling people about this. You know?... in outrage for our brother Mumia, that they would take this kind of position.

We're saying every day this government shows you how insane it is.

It is *out of control*. We cannot expect those who are out of control to behave as if they are in control. *We* have to bring them back into control.

We've got to do that.

[Audience applauds]

Those who have some sense and who can see the insanity in this... it's *our* work to put things right. And this begins by understanding the value of our own power of purpose, and understanding that we cannot look to, we cannot elect or select, somebody else to do our thinking for us... to coordinate our lives for us... to tell us what we should be doing or shouldn't do... how we should raise our families... all of that stuff. We have to do that ourselves.

And that's evident when you look around you and look at the people that we are *supposed* to be getting all of this direction and guidance and support from.

The Governator[14] is going to tell you how to... [audience becomes agitated and vocal]...live your life? He's going to tell you what's best for you?

---

14 Arnold Schwarzenegger, who was governor of California at the time. It refers to his well-known movie role as the Terminator.

George Bush[15]... is going to give you some direction about your life, your family life, how you should be living your life? This man can't even keep up with his own two daughters. What's he gonna do for you?

What's he gonna do for you?

When Bill Clinton was courting people so that he could get elected president, he pledged his loyalty, his understanding to people. He told people that he was going to give you a better life.. he was going to take care of you... he was going to look out for you... all of that. But when he was courting Hillary, he told her the same thing.

[Audience laughs loudly and claps]

And he didn't mean it... he didn't mean it any more when he said it to her then when he said it to you, because he don't even know you. He know her. He don't even know you.

So, how many examples do we need to understand that we can't look to these people for anything? ...that we have a brain and our head that we supposed to use?

If the God of life... the Mother of life didn't want you thinking for yourself and coordinating your own life, why put a brain in your head? Why not just give a brain to George Bush and let him do the thinking for everybody?

That's not how it is. Everybody has a brain in their head to use... to coordinate your own life... to think for yourself.

That is what we have to do. Revolution starts with self... with self.

[Audience applauds]

Now, we got a whole lot of front-line soldiers who are sitting in these prisons... unjustly... because of the system. They have put their lives, their freedom, on the line for the people. Not for themselves. Not for themselves.

If Mumia, if Leonard, if Sundiata [Acoli][16], if Mutulu [Shakur][17], the

---

15 George W. Bush, U.S. president at the time.
16 Sundiata Acoli (born 1937) is a political activist who was a member of the Black Panther Party and the Black Liberation Army. He was sentenced to life in prison in 1974 and was granted parole in 2022 at the age of 85.
17 Mutulu Shakur (1950-2023) was an activist and member of the Black Liberation Army, sentenced to sixty years

MOVE 9, Marilyn [Buck], Dylcia Pagán... all of these freedom fighters, political prisoners and former political prisoners... if they were only concerned about themselves, they wouldn't be imprisoned because they'd just be going about their business, living their lives. And they wouldn't *care* about changing things to make life better for people.

But they do care. We all care. And they put their lives on the line for us.

They're not telling you to put your life on the line... to be on the front line. They're saying, "We got that. But do your part."

Do whatever it is that you can do in this revolution for yourself... for your own freedom... not for them... for yourself... for your family... for your babies. You know?

We don't want to see nobody else's baby *bombed* and burned alive. We don't wanna see another Amadou Diallo.[18]

We don't want anybody else sitting on death row because of this *rotten system*.

We don't want to see that.

But, if you don't want to see that, we've got to do the work to make sure it doesn't happen.

Now, you can work on what ever level you can. If you have a 9-to-5 handiwork in an office and you have access to a computer or a photocopier, *use* it for this revolution.

Design a flyer. Send out emails. Photocopy information. You know?

If you are a parent or parents that have young children, get together with other parents of young children and work together so that you can take turns watching the kids and you can all be a little more allowed to work together.

If you have a vehicle... and you know that people are working their behinds off... and some people don't have a vehicle and need to get information or literature or pick up things or whatever you can offer your services to drive

---

in prison for his involvement in 1981. In November 2022, the U.S. Parole Commission granted Shakur's release on parole. He was the stepfather of Tupac Shakur.

18 Amadou Diallo was murdered by the New York Police Department on February 4, 1999. See the interview with Amadou Diallo's mother on page 64.

people around when you have a little time. Or offer them your car if you comfortable with that. Do that.

If you like to cook... if you're just somebody that likes to cook and you're into nutrition and health, or you simply like to cook... When there's things going on... big programs going on, the people are working from sunup to sundown and going half the day or all day without eating... cook some food and bring it to where people are working and feed them. You know? Feed them.

You could be the most bourgeois person in the world. You could have your Louis Vuitton shoes and handbag, and your Versace dresses, and your hair perfectly coiffed, and your nails out to here [indicates fingernails about six inches long] with diamond chips in them.

If that's your thing then that's your thing. But if you got a good heart and you know that things are not right and want to do something, get together with your friends and put on a fashion show or something and *raise some money*.

Do *something*.

[Audience applauds and whistles]

Do *something*.

Just like it is a crime... a sin to oppress, enslave, and exploit, it is JUST as much a crime, a sin *not* to fight those things... *not* to work to free yourself from those things.

[Audience applauds]

It is *just* as much a crime.

So, if you don't take anything else away from here tonight, take that one thing with you, that if you didn't know before, doggone it, you know it now... that you are *obligated* to do *something* in this fight for freedom, whatever it is.

[Audience applauds]

Nobody else can do your work for you. I can do *my* work. But I can't do yours. You see?

I cannot eat and fill your stomach.

I cannot drink and quench your thirst.

I can't do it.

I cannot sleep and have you feel rested.

You've got to do that for yourself.

And that principle applies across the board.

That's why things are in such bad shape now... because people have been tricked into thinking that somebody else can carry their weight for them... that you can pay somebody or elect or select somebody to do your work for you.

Can't happen.

Can't happen.

Nothin' but trouble there. Nothin' but trouble.

That's a message that I hope you get tonight.

My family, the MOVE 9... actually there are eight people now. My sister Merle Africa was killed in prison in 1998. First they said from natural causes. Then they said she had tumors in her body that travelled to her lungs and stopped her breathing. Then they said she had cancer... I mean, they kept changing the story.

We don't believe any of it. Merle was a strong, healthy MOVE woman. To just suddenly die like that, with nothing preceding it... something is wrong. Something is *definitely* wrong there.

So now, it's eight MOVE members. Their appeals are in the first level of the Federal district court. We are not looking to the courts for any justice or miracles.

We know that our people and all political prisoners' way home is through the people, *not* through the courts.

That does not mean that we don't file the available appeals. We do, because we know that when the pressure from the people *forces* the system to release our people, there's got to be a mechanism there for them to do it.

So, we filed the appeals, but we concentrate our energy on the people... on the people, because *that* is where the power is.

At this point, the only thing that people need to do is be aware, get informed, get information, and figure out what it is that you can do to carry some weight here... to carry your own weight here. Because, see, when everybody is working for freedom, for justice, for what is right, then that's a *strong* vibration and everybody's moving in the same direction. And there *ain't* no stopping us when we *unify*.

You see, some people can do it. But that's like a few raindrops... individual raindrops falling. But when those raindrops turn into a monsoon, then you got some *power* there. And that's what we have to be – the monsoon, not individual raindrops.

So, let's get busy. Let's get to work. Let's get on the move. And *stay* on the move...on the move.

Long live the MOVE 9. Long live Mumia. Long live Leonard Peltier, Marilyn Buck, the Puerto Rican Independistas. Long live the Zapatistas. Long live those indigenous grandmothers at Big Mountain in Arizona. Long live those who are fighting for freedom and for their lives in Vieques. Long live Earth First!, the Earth Liberation Front, the Animal Liberation Front. Long live *all freedom fighters*... all those who love freedom enough to fight for it.

LONG LIVE THE SPIRIT OF RESISTANCE!

[Audience applauds and whistles loudly]

LONG LIVE REVOLUTION!

LONG LIVE JOHN AFRICA!

DOWN WITH THIS ROTTEN-ASS SYSTEM!

ON THE MOVE!

[Audience continues to applaud and whistle continuously for about a minute]

Sacajawea ('Saki') Hall

"Saki" Hall is a radical Black feminist activist, mother, birth-worker, educator and journalist who loves crafting. She sees her life's work as engaging in the collective struggle for Afrikan liberation, human rights and social transformation. She is a native Lower East Side New Yorker who migrated to Jackson, Mississippi in December 2013 to help advance the Jackson-Kush Plan. She is a founding member of Cooperation Jackson. Interviewed by Thandisizwe Chimurenga about the intersection of gender justice and the solidarity economy at Cooperation Jackson.

• • •

Thandisizwe Chimurenga: I see in one of your bios you talk about growing up in a solidarity economy, having a cooperative upbringing, what do you mean by that?

Saki Hall: Yes, once I began learning and actively working on the various aspects of our program here in Jackson towards building worker-owned cooperatives, time-banking and bartering structure, housing cooperatives, a community land trust, etc., I began to see my work with Cooperation Jackson as a reflection of my lived experience.

My mother is from Haiti and my father is from St. Louis, Missouri. Since I lived in New York with my mom's side of the family, the Haitian side of my family predominantly raised me. So I have my Haitian family and then my extended family of friends I grew up with living in the Lower East Side of Manhattan. Both were tight-knit communities. In both cases we didn't have a lot of money so folks creatively figured out how to meet their needs. I feel like I was raised in two cultures that actually taught me some of the fundamentals of what it means to care and share with each other, to be a cooperator, as they say in the cooperative world. Caring and sharing is a key dimension of solidarity.

My mom has told me a story several times of when my dad bartered a painting for bread. He had done a small oil painting of a loaf of bread with a wine bottle based on a local bakery. One day they were hungry and had no money, so he went to the bakery and in exchange for the painting the baker gave him the same daily baked long loaf of bread featured my dad's painting. At that time they lived on about $800 a month with only a VA pension and an SSI check.

In New York City, during the 1980s we used subway tokens in place of dollars at bodegas – a corner store – and with street vendors. My best friend and I stretched our resources on Saturdays by going through together with one token each way on the subway and then we'd have two tokens to use for lunch. So, we could share a hot dog and a knish[1] from a hot dog vendor.

Another example that connects me to the work I'm doing now is the apartment building I grew up in on East 9th Street. My mother gave birth to me and my father delivered me in our apartment in 1978 with everyone from the building there pitching in. Our building went through a long coop conversion process. It was residents self-managed through the 1980s and then formally became a low-income co-op in the early 1990s. I had always known we had a tenant association that governed and managed the buildings; I did not know that I lived in a "shared-equity cooperative" until two years ago at a Community Land Trust conference I went to for Cooperation Jackson. After college I learned of the strong housing, homesteading and squatting movements that the Lower East Side had, along with other boroughs like the Bronx. My building was a product of the successful actions and organizing. Now I'm learning the details of the process on a deeper level 'cause I'm one of the people leading similar work in CJ around housing.

---

1 Eastern European snack food consisting of a filling covered with dough that is either baked, grilled, or deep fried. Knishes can be purchased from street vendors in urban areas with a large Jewish population, sometimes at a hot dog stand or from a butcher shop. It was made popular in North America by Eastern European immigrants from the Pale of Settlement (mainly from present-day Belarus, Poland, Lithuania and Ukraine).

What these stories mean for me in terms of our work in Jackson is that I've come to realize, remember really, that I have lived experiences that show what we are aiming for is possible. A major part of my Cooperation Jackson work is land and housing, developing the Fannie Lou Hamer Community Land Trust with the goal of creating cooperative housing. So it is totally possible for us to have quality, affordable housing, which is a human right. And even more importantly, we can collectively own and control the land and our housing. We are asserting that we have a right to the city here in Jackson.

We have the human right to remain where we are, where people have been for generations. Especially in the South where the roots are generations upon generations deep. I feel like I've come full circle, and we are working to take it to another level. Our work is about moving away from land and housing as a commodity to be bought and sold to the highest bidder. It is a human right violation for a single woman and her family to be kicked out of an apartment because they can't afford the rent anymore. Because of how cheap land is in Jackson, development plans like expanding the medical corridor, the West Jackson Master plan, possibly a domed sports complex, stand to make huge profits. Black people in poor and working class neighborhoods stand to be displaced, it's the kind of mass displacement happening across the U.S. in Oakland, Chicago, New Orleans, Atlanta, D.C. That's why we are putting in place the tool of a community land trust that protects the land from corporate developers and puts the development process in the hands of the community that collectively owns and controls the land.

From my childhood to now, I see the creativity of everyday working people and their organic practice of solidarity, especially women of color, immigrant women, single women, the women I grew up with including my mother. So we have a responsibility to: a) recognize and value that, and b) tap into the creativity and practices that already exist to strengthen and expand it. And connect it to a movement for transformative liberation.

I think our vision and goals resonate with people. I think a lot of people have a similar experience like I'm describing. So many of us have these roots that have been passed down in most ways informally. Black people would not have survived the brutality of chattel slavery and Jim Crow apartheid without practicing solidarity and cooperation in organized formal ways.

So it is that sharing, caring and cooperation from the past with the ways we continue to do that now to survive we want to very intentionally tap into and make it systematic with formal institutions like time banks, skill shares, bartering and a dynamic solidarity economy.

TC: You identify as a Black feminist.

SH: Right, a radical Black feminist.

TC: How do Black feminist politics and the struggle for Black women's liberation connect with the work of Cooperation Jackson and the effort to build the solidarity economy?

SH: Now, I didn't know about the concepts, theories and ideologies of radical social transformation growing up that I do now, I didn't know for example what being an anti-capitalist meant, although from a very early age I questioned why some people could have so much and others have so little. With my visits to Haiti and going to middle school outside of my neighborhood, I remember grappling with how it made no sense to me when I could see plenty of resources, and that if we wanted to we could spread resources equally to everyone. I remember talking to the same best friend who I shared tokens with, about this using a car analogy. I thought instead of a person having a Lexus and someone else not having a car that we could all be driving around in Hondas [laughter]. You know, so I was thinking of ways to redistribute wealth in middle school before I know of the term redistribution of wealth.

So growing up in the 'hood, Black, a child of an immigrant, in a diverse multi- national, working class neighborhood, I formed a race and class analysis early on, my gender analysis did not get fully shaped until later.

For me, women have to be at the center of our efforts to build a solidarity economy. So when I talk about that organic solidarity I grew up with, the informal ways oppressed people around the world live and work cooperatively, even the so-called informal economy, women are at the center of that.

Again, using an example from my childhood, I remember being sent downstairs to borrow milk, sugar or some other food on the regular. It's not borrowing 'cause you can't give what you put in some cereal and ate back [laughter]. We didn't have to pay anyone back because they came to our house just the same. And when I think about it, 9 times out of 10 it had to do with cooking and meals, and the majority of the time it was women doing that cooking. So I took part in that mutual aid, now what I didn't know and learned recently when my godmother passed away, was that they shared food stamps. And mind you I know people exchanged food stamps as a form of currency. When I heard that I was like wow, that's deep, I actually wrote it down on the, you know, the program they have at wakes. Learning that women shared food stamps spoke volumes to me about women. We are creative about how to take care of our families and each other with very little resources.

I'm sharing that example because what I take from it is how central "care work" is to the practice of solidarity. And if we are going to truly build a solidarity economy that is transformative, women have to be at the center of that. In Cooperation Jackson we recognize this. As an organization, we are working towards fully recognizing care work, and fully center it as much as we center the value of worker cooperatives in building a solidarity economy.

Women pretty much still take on the primary responsibility for care work. This work holds the social fabric of communities together and labor goes into creating or reproducing this fabric every day, social reproduction. Care work includes maintaining a household, parenting children, taking care of a grandparent, taking care of other people's family, social activities, healing, cooking, emotional support, even sex. A radical feminist lens recognizes social reproduction as labor and care work is critical to social reproduction. Capitalism and patriarchy separate social reproduction from economic production. It makes a false separation between public and private. Social reproductive labor is not valued, recognized, it's unpaid, in some cases paid but severely underpaid. Disconnecting social reproduction from economic production marginalizes the people who do social reproductive labor, making their role invisible and easily exploited.

Any economy relies on social production. Capitalism would not survive without social reproductive labor, the unpaid labor that allows for immense profit. What would profit margins be if a company had to pay the husband for working in the office and his wife for the work she does to run their home? Or had to pay a single mom double for her 9-to-5 and her care work? Domestic workers, mostly non-white women, mostly immigrants, work for low pay, do unpaid care work at home, and with the sheer amount of hours taking care of someone's family and home, it limits the time they can provide for their family and community.

Sex workers are in the public and private sphere, doing paid work that is criminalized because socially it's for the private sphere and morally only for married hetero men and women.

So social reproduction and the role of women, and some men, is solidarity based, and a solidarity economy can reflect and support the transformation of society, a solidarity economy in and of itself doesn't automatically end gender and sexual oppression. But it does offer an opportunity unlike capitalism.

For Cooperation Jackson we believe we have to challenge ourselves and each other to actively struggle against patriarchy and heterosexism in our work and in our lives. Assigned gender roles and norms that dictate who is a woman, what being a man means, even the subtle things like what color is allowed for which gender, pink being for girls and blue being for boys. Violence that comes in different forms is used to enforce these made-up concepts, especially towards people who do not conform to these standards like transgender people.

I see it as my responsibility as a member of Cooperation Jackson, as a mother, as a birth worker, to provide a Black radical feminist analysis for our work and to push us all towards practice that is beyond theory. And that is the hard part.

The multiple systems of oppression and how they overlap limit us all.

TC: Cooperation Jackson is working on participatory budgeting. What would it look like if Black women were in charge of the budget or had a say in the city budget? Is fighting for a participatory budget an intentional part of the work of Cooperation Jackson in terms of integrating Black women's knowledge and experiences into how to govern a municipality? Is that part of the plan?

SH: We've been talking about and studying participatory and human rights budgeting. Which in simple terms is creating a budget that actually comes out of the community and reflects its needs, as opposed to a budget that is created by government officials and then we all deal with the consequences of it. In Jackson, Mississippi, if Black women, especially Black working-class women, were centered in the process of creating a budget, I think it would look very different than the city's typical budget. What I mean by centered is that the development of a budget would be driven by the knowledge, experience, ideas and participation of Black women. For example, I think education and schools, things like affordable housing would be prioritized compared to police departments or tourism. So it would be important for families like mine that have a hard time or cannot pay at all for extra-curricular activities to have access to free afterschool programs, free arts programs, that could be included in a city budget. Going back to housing like I talked about earlier, the priority placed on urban redevelopment often means giving tax breaks to corporate developers.

I'm sure for poor and working-class women, bringing in money to help improve the city wouldn't mean displacing them from their homes. Protecting affordable housing with policy and the money to back it up would be my priority if I had a part in the planning.

The city of Jackson is in a budget crisis; so hard decisions have to be made about what gets cut, where money goes and how much goes where. If we were able to do things differently, these decisions would be based on the people most directly impacted. So, in our case setting priorities for Jackson's urgent infrastructure repairs would be done in a democratic participatory process set through the lens of Black and other working class people, particularly women and not the contractors and the corporations that typically dominate the process and its outcomes.

The important part is actually how decisions get made, not only about allocating resources through a budget, it is about who is there to make those decisions, how much power do they have and can use in the process. So, yeah there's a lot of things that are needed, that have to be changed on the municipal level for us to get to the goals we set outlined in the Jackson-Kush Plan that relate to human rights or participatory budgeting, and more. There are a lot of things that have to change to create a deep democratic system. Human rights budgeting is just one of the tools that will go a long way towards advancing our goals. That is why we've been studying it and plan to relaunch mass education and trainings on human rights budgeting. Not only is there an opportunity to meet the economic and social needs going unmet when the decision makers don't have the same interest, – imagine the impact of the process with practicing agency and collective power through the process.

TC: When I hear people say women in leadership it makes me think of a woman, a female figurehead. When I hear about women's participation, what comes to mind are women doing the majority of the work, but not receiving the credit or acknowledgement of their work. So women already participate, women are in leadership. You know to me it's more than women and leadership or women's participation. How is this being practiced in Cooperation Jackson?

SH: Right, women's leadership has to be centered, it is not enough to have us in the room. To me there is a difference between women having roles in an organization and women having power in an organization. When I say power I mean decision-making power that sets the agenda and goals of every dimension of the organization.

Audre Lorde[2] is quoted often saying we don't live single-issue lives and there is no hierarchy of oppression. That highlights the intersectionality framework that informs our work. Cooperation Jackson politically understands that Black people's self-determination and liberation is not possible without ending heteropatriarchy just like it is not possible without ending capitalism and white supremacy.

Radical feminism recognizes the intersections of heterosexism, patriarchy, capitalism, white supremacy, and other systems of oppression. These systems of oppression privilege men, privilege heterosexuals, privileges whiteness, privileges the ruling class, English as a language, adults, etc. In Cooperation Jackson we have a vision of a deep democratic, cooperative, sustainable community. For us that means we have to create a culture free of patriarchy and heterosexism. Our struggles are connected and our liberation is intrinsically connected and we are committed to moving us as close as possible in that direction.

I like this analogy, written in an article by a queer Jewish man. I almost didn't read it, the title got me though, and it turned out to be a pretty

---

2 Audre Lorde (1934-1992) was a Black lesbian feminist poet, writer, and activist. Her work often explored themes of identity, intersectionality, and social justice, and she was known for her powerful and incisive critiques of racism, sexism, homophobia, and other forms of oppression.

damn good article. Anyway, he says oppression operates like a wheel with all these spokes representing our marginalized identities. I was glad when I got to the part where he wrote about intersectional privilege using his overlapping privilege and not only his overlapping oppression. Right, so I like it for that reason and he says that if you only focus on breaking your spoke then the wheel keeps going on rolling over people. So of course I was in total agreement reading him say to reach true lasting liberation we have to dismantle all of the spokes in all the shapes and forms they take. He didn't give a visual description of it, but I could see spokes breaking and the wheel slowly losing its speed and falling because the structure of it is gone.

So back to Cooperation Jackson specifically, like every organization, at least that I'm aware of, we are struggling to create this liberated space in our organization and we all know we have a long way to go in our communities.

What we have done to this point is that we've institutionalized space for women's leadership and queer leadership. I'm excited that our membership and core leadership of the organization represents young queer people and women. That stands out in Jackson, Mississippi [chuckle]. At the same time, that is not enough. Heterosexist views and behaviors have to be struggled with and shifted. We attempt to make tasks non-gendered like taking notes at a meeting and cleaning. It is interesting how we all fall into defaults and have to remind ourselves and each other.

Patriarchy is a- hell of a ... [pause]

TC: Well, hell of a drug!

SH: [laughs] Yeah, and so you know, it rears its ugly head in the personal and political spaces. Even in radical, progressive, women-friendly, queer-friendly spaces, time and time again. And we've internalized it, so even women and queer folks perpetuate it ourselves.

We have been intentional in actively creating the space and environment that is truly open and conducive to women and queer folks coming in from anywhere and genuinely feeling like they can fully engage and participate in discussing the work and doing the work. And it is in subtle and overt ways. Like having a sign that says, "gender is a universe" on our bathroom door that was posted on a cute post. We have a banner on our entrance wall outside that says, "All Our Family Welcomed", with the rainbow and gender equality symbols including a combined queer and Black power symbol. We have a room called the little people's society named by one of our members. She is a high school student and her family provides childcare at our gatherings. Little people (children) are welcome in all spaces is a community agreement.

TC: What do you see going forward?

SH: So, I think the question you raised is really, really important. And as a leader of Cooperation Jackson, I have to make sure that we create the time and space to engage in the struggle to dismantle sexism, patriarchy, and heterosexism. Because it takes time, it takes processing. It's about our relationships with each other. So, I'm not the only one doing this, but it can't only be a few of us. I do see it as part of my responsibility though, to point out when sexist language or behavior happens, or to highlight the impact on women if we are talking about an issue and that gets left out. And that can be uncomfortable and frustrating at times.

Cooperation Jackson has to systematize these things, document this analysis and integrate it into all of our writing more. We need to document how it is impacting our work and practice, both successes and challenges.

A challenge for me is how to encourage and push the younger women in the organization to be more visible and vocal in our overall work. But I have to check myself sometimes because it can't only be about the way I define active leadership or challenging patriarchy. So, I am constantly learning and developing myself, which is a part of the process, unpacking our privilege and unlearning what we've been socialized to accept.

What I think we have done is create the space for this to happen, instead of sitting back and waiting for them to ask to step into a role, we are encouraging and asking them to facilitate a meeting, do a report back. Collective models of leadership and decision-making can provide a space for everyone to participate fully. But it has to be coupled with principles and practices like men stepping back and not dominating discussions, sharing power overall. So I see us getting stronger in our theory and practice.

Samaria Rice

Tamir Rice was 12 years old when he was gunned down by an incompetent Cleveland police officer November 22, 2014, while playing with a toy gun in a local park. Tamir's mother, Samaria Rice, was approached briefly during the annual Oscar Grant Foundation banquet in Hayward, CA, on February 27, 2016.

• • •

Thandisizwe Chimurenga: So, first of all, I'm so sorry for your loss.

Samaria Rice: Yes.

TC: I'm not going to take too much time. I just want to know, what is it that you want people to know?

SR: I want people to know that Tamir was a baby, and he was 12 years old, and how can you diminish a 12-year-old's character? It's sad that in America, my son can't even play with a toy BB gun in the park, and you know, boys will be boys. You know what I'm saying? It was given to him by a friend. It wasn't like it was his own. Shame on the Cleveland Police Department for letting Timothy Loehmann, who was the shooting officer, and Frank Gramback, the officer that drove the vehicle – shame on them that, you know, they didn't approach the situation or at least try to assess the situation before they took my child's life.

TC: That's what you want people to know?

SR: Yeah. I mean, it's a lot. It's a lot I want them to know.

TC: What's the most important thing that you think people should know?

SR: I'm fighting for justice for Tamir and all our stolen lives out here. America definitely needs to do better, and it's gonna take all of us together to fix this problem, and it could start there. I definitely want accountability for my child, and it could start there, far as accountability with the officer. That would give me peace, if the officer can go to jail. The healing process could start there, and I think that would be for a lot of our mothers out here that's in this struggle. We want accountability for our babies. How do they think we're supposed to sleep at night while they keep on employing the same officers to different counties and different cities? That's not going to work. They need to be gone off the force forever, you know what I'm saying? Forever, especially when they committing crimes like that. And it's sad on the government's part, you know, it's just sad on their part that they allowing them to just assassinate us like we're dogs in the street, So, yeah. And I'm fighting for justice, and I'm not gonna stop fighting.

SR: My name is Samaria Rice. I'm the mother of Tamir Rice. They need to know me, baby!

TC: Thank you.

SR: You're welcome.

Black Women's Health

Byllye Avery and Iyanla Vanzant on Forgiveness

The Black Women's Health Imperative is "the first nonprofit organization created by Black women to help protect and advance the health and wellness of Black women and girls," focusing on the areas of health policy, research, knowledge and leadership development and communications. This conversation was recorded October 9, 2008, as part of the Imperative's 25th-anniversary celebration; an audio-teleconference/conversation with/between Byllye Y. Avery, MacArthur Genius award winner, author and founder of the Black Women's Health Imperative, and world-renowned spiritual teacher, inspirational speaker and author Iyanla Vanzant, on forgiveness and emotional well-being. This conversation is based on a chapter of Ms. Vanzant's Tapping The Power Within: A Path to Self Empowerment for Women *(20th anniversary edition).*

• • •

Byllye Avery: First of all, I want to welcome Sister Iyanla to our conference call. And I want to congratulate you on this wonderful 20th-anniversary edition. It is a wonderful day when this kind of thing happens. Your first edition of *Tapping The Power Within* has pretty much become a Bible among African American women. You see people with it everywhere, you see people using it. And I was just having a conversation with one of my colleagues the other day about the upcoming program we're doing today. And she was saying how she uses the "forgiveness diet" in her work. And it has been a wonderful gift that you've given to us. And I personally want to thank you, my sister.

Iyanla Vanzant: Oh, you are so welcome. And thank you for inviting me into the conversation today.

BA: Oh, yes, it's great. Now, we are facing some very, very difficult times some, we've got an election going on[1] that we are all working real hard in. The whole world seems to be in a crisis. We're facing, on top of everything else, the worst economic downturn since the Great Depression.[2] And who knows we might be almost going into the Great Depression. And I know that this is such a stressful time for us. And for us as Black women, we live stressed *live* anyway, just trying to live in this society when things seem to be working all right. And I know that this is gonna be a really difficult time. So before we start out a conversation about forgiveness or all leading into it, however you want to do it, please say some words to us and give us some wisdom as to how we can start to deal with our fears and our worries, and embrace whatever we need to do to get through this.

IV: The first thing I would say to everybody who's listening, I don't know where everyone is, I happen to be sitting in my office and there's a tree outside of my office. So I would say to everybody right where they are right now to just stop and find something to focus on. Maybe a picture of a loved one, maybe a plant. If you have a window, just look outside the window and just fix your focus and your concentration on something. Particularly or specifically something living if you have it. If not something that opens your heart up, just stop what you're doing. And look at that thing. While you're looking at it, just become aware of your breath, your inhale and your exhale, just become aware of it. You don't need to do anything the breath will breathe. As you're focusing on that object, whatever it is, focusing on your breath, just listen for a second. Just listen.

You can hear the sound of my voice. You can hear the hum in the phone. You can hear whatever is going on around you. Just listen. What I also want you to notice that in your focus and in your breathing is absolutely nothing you need in this moment. Nothing you need. In this moment you're not too much of anything; too big, too old, too young, nothing.

---

1 The 2008 U.S. elections were held on November 4. Democratic Senator Barack Obama of Illinois won the presidential election, defeating his challenger, Senator John McCain, by a wide margin, and the Democrats bolstered their majorities in both chambers of Congress.

2 A period of marked general decline was observed in national economies globally, i.e. a recession, that occurred from late 2007 to 2009. At the time, the International Monetary Fund (IMF) concluded that it was the most severe economic and financial meltdown since the Great Depression.

Just focus and breathe and listen. And this level of stillness, this level of peace we can have every single day regardless of what's going on around us. It's a question of focus. It's a question of breath. And it's a question of listening. Now imagine if we did this, just stopped and did this, two or three times a day. We wouldn't be shaken by the external events, we would have a sense of peace and calm within. And whatever we need to know, we will know. And it's just that simple, Byllye. You focus and you're breathing, and you're listening. What I would say, is make it a priority, to take moments out of your day, to just get still, as your quiet time, quiet time with yourself, your quiet time with God. Now, if you were to drop into that moment, just a word, or a scripture, or something inspirational. You know, I'm a student of *A Course in Miracles*. And every day I read my course. And every day, the lesson gives me something. And today's lesson says, "My heart is beating in the peace of God." That's today's lesson. Surrounding me is all the life that God created in His love. It calls to me in every heartbeat, and in every breath, and every action, and every thought piece fills my heart. So its simple.

BA: Yes, thank you so much for helping us create that oasis. And that's a wonderful space that we can go to. I'm here gazing on a bamboo plant that gave me so much, just in those moments.

IV: Bamboo is long life and bamboo is sturdy. Bamboo is strength, you know. So the other thing we have to do is make sure that wherever we are in whatever environment we're in, whether the office, the home, the bathroom, wherever we are, that we have that sacred place that we can go to, to get still to breathe, to focus, and to make sure that there's something living in that thing.

BA: Asé. Now talk to us about forgiveness. What is it and how important is it?

IV: Well, I frequently say to people that forgiveness is your "spiritual laxative." If you want to clean out your mind. If you want to clean out your your body, if you want to clean out your, your, your emotional being, you know, just like we would take Ex-lax or a colon cleanser to clean out our physical self. Forgiveness is the the medication if you will, that cleans you out. It cleans out memories, it cleans out perceptions, it cleans out beliefs, it clears out feelings, it's a clearing. And the same way that we frequently have to take or get support in terms of cleaning out our body, whether we're fasting or, or we are on some form of herbal supplement just to clean out our body, we need to do the same thing with forgiveness so that we don't get clogged. We don't become toxic. We don't become constipated, if you will, with negative emotions and negative memory.

BA: And there is so much out there to keep us constantly constipated.

IV: Oh yeah, many of us are emotionally and spiritually constipated. We can't move off one spot on one thought on one belief, because you know, everything is backed up and clogged up and our pipes are corroded, if you will.

BA: Right. And to clean out those pipes will be a good thing because it can help you feel good. Because some of us have been feeling bad for so long. We don't know what feeling good is.

IV: Yeah. And in fact, some of us are afraid to feel good, because we're waiting for the next shoe to fall.

BA: Yeah, always waiting for the next, can't even enjoy the moment now. Hmm. Something just might happen. And "if I relax for half a second something is going to fall."

IV: That's right.

BA: Yeah. But that whole cleansing process feels like such a good thing. Such a good thing. Well, what happens to us, those of us who can't figure out forgiving and when we don't forgive when we want to hold on to something forever?

IV: Well I don't think that it's that we want to hold on, I think that many of us believe we need to hold on because of the wrongness or the unfairness or the impropriety, inappropriateness, of whatever the action was towards us whether we were violated as children or abandoned or rejected or had our hearts broken. You know, we want to hold that person accountable and responsible for their behavior. And absolutely, they should be accountable and responsible for their behavior. It may just not be to us. One of the things that I talk about in *Tapping the Power Within* is that everything in life is a lesson. Whatever it is, and when lessons come to you, you're either teaching a lesson, learning a lesson, or the object by which the lesson is being taught. And sometimes you could be minding your own business and something or someone will come into your world and just behave badly, leaving you, you know, emotionally scarred or damaged. And in those times you have to say, "Okay, what am I learning here?" Or, "How was I an object?" You know, there's an old hymn that says, "God uses ordinary people." Sometimes you're somebody's teacher, the way they behave in your life sets up a lesson for them. Sometimes you're the object that God will use to bring people to an awareness of how they need to shift or change. And, and it's really a function of love. Just as the reading said today, you know, "God's love be in my heart." And God loves us all, and all of us to get what we need. And sometimes it takes a real traumatic event, because for some reason human beings learn best by pain.

BA: Really, really. "No pain no gain."

IV: We learn best by pain, you know? We don't pay attention until it hurts. We don't pay attention.

BA: Right. You know, my mother used to say to me, if you don't learn this lesson, you will repeat it until you get it. Once you learn it you will not be presented it anymore.

IV: That's right. Absolutely.

BA: Yes. That was one of her things. One of her sermons, that was the one, you have to get the lesson, you have to get it.

You talk about a "spiritual curriculum" in your book. How do you prepare yourself for this lesson?

IV: You are born. You know, that curriculum is set in your soul before you even get here. There's one of my favorite scriptures that says, "When you were being shaped and formed in your mother's womb, I knew you." Yeah. So our Creator knows who we are, knows what we've come here to learn. And those lessons are what we call the spiritual curriculum. And from the time you are born, everything from whether you're nursed or bottle fed, really, from the time you're in the womb, let me give you an example if I can:

My mother was an alcoholic. And so I marinated. Not only was she an alcoholic, my father was married, she was the other woman. So what I've learned about myself, is that I marinated in an environment of alcohol, shame, guilt. That's what I marinated in. So coming into this life, I've had many experiences where I've had to overcome shame and guilt. Many,

many instances, you know that, and both of those toxic emotions, you know, diminish my value and my worth, there was always something I was afraid of, ashamed of, my behavior engendered shame and fear and guilt. And so what I learned, many, many years later, was that was my curriculum, to learn how to behave in such a way that I didn't create it for myself, that I didn't allow other people to heap it upon me. And then to build up my value, esteem and worth, to build up myself.

And the funny thing is my, because my mother drank, I have never drank in my life. I don't drink. Never have. And my aunt used to say that's because your mother kept you drunk when you were in the womb.

BA: Well whatever, it worked.

IV: You know? So what happens is we're born with certain propensities. The same way we inherit eyes, ears, nose, mouth, we inherit certain emotional and spiritual and, and psychological propensities. And that is what we call our curriculum. And our job in life is to master those lessons.

BA: Absolutely. And to be brave enough to go back and and claim and name, and name the things that happened to you so that you can see how to unravel or how to develop your curriculum. You got to do it.

IV: It's not even to unravel them. It's just to acknowledge them. Acknowledge them is the first, acknowledgement is the first step towards healing. Until we can acknowledge what happened without blame or projection, without holding anybody responsible. Or holding anybody hostage, I won't say responsible, I will say hostage because everybody's responsible for what they do. But if we would stop holding people responsible and look at the experience, and ask the right questions. One of the things about, you know, forgiveness, it helps us because so very often, we don't ask the right question. We'll say, "Why did this happen to me?" Well, why not? Here's a better question. "What was I learning?" "Or what can I learn? From what happened to me?" "How can I use this experience to make myself a better person?" Those are more appropriate questions than "Why did you do this? Why did this happen?"

BA: Right. So we're really given all of those tools right there. We just need to know how to use them appropriately in a way that informs our growth.

IV: Yes.

BA: Informs our growth. Well, you know, some of us are trapped in a cycle of negativity, we just like, seem to be swirling in it, you know?

IV: "Negaholics"

BA: Right right "negaholics"! Yeah, right now, you know, how do we break loose and, and forgive and release? Talk us through a process of that.

IV: The first thing you have to do is know that forgiveness is your tool. Forgiveness is a skill. Forgiveness is a gift to yourself, that's the first thing you have to do. And don't think in terms of right and wrong, we have to eliminate that whole concept of right and wrong, because those are judgments. We have to think in terms of *is*. This is what is, this is the reality of what has happened or what I feel or what went on, this is the reality. And anytime you argue with reality, you will suffer. If you say this should not have happened, they should not have done this, she/he should have done the other then you're arguing with reality, because that is not what happened.

So the first thing I would say is, you got to get clear about your reality. What happened? How do you feel about it? Who was involved? Not whether they should have or shouldn't have been, but what is the reality. Then we have to embrace another concept that's very, very challenging for us. And that is that no matter what you have experienced physically, mentally, or emotionally, I don't care what, it has not changed the core of your being, it has not touched your spirit. It has not harmed you, at the essence, the basis of who you are. So we have to think beyond the physicality. And we have to say "this has not changed me, it has made an impression and impact, but it has not changed me." And once we can do that, once we can understand that we haven't been changed by this, ut's changed our thoughts, perhaps it's changed our emotions. But it hasn't changed the core and the essence of who we are. That place that we tap into when we focus and breathe, then what we have to do is acknowledge our thoughts about the experience.

So I was sexually abused as a child. And my thoughts about that was, it was wrong, he shouldn't have, I should have been protected, and bla bla bla, but none of that happened. So I was sexually violated as a child. And now I have my tools for forgiveness. Right? And what am I forgiving? Well, the master's degree in forgiveness comes from going to yourself first. So I forgive myself for believing that I should not have been violated as a child. Because I was, I was. So how can I say I shouldn't have been? It happened? Yeah. So I can't argue with reality. I forgive myself for believing that my uncle was wrong. Now that's the master's level. Most of us, many of us need to start at the basic level, which would be I forgive my uncle for sexually violating me as a child. I forgive my aunt for not protecting me from my uncle, you know, the elementary, the basic level is to project it outward. But what you'll discover is if you do that, and you do a thorough job of it, ultimately, it will come back to you. Either way will work right, either way.

And we also, in the midst of that, I have to realize that sometimes some of that protection didn't come because it couldn't come. If it could have, it would have. And then we expect people to protect us who couldn't protect themselves. Quite often.

We expect people to honor us when they weren't honoring themselves, expect people to give to us what they couldn't give to themselves. One would think that a grown man would know how to honor and respect and give appropriate love and affection to a young girl. But we also don't know what his curriculum is.

BA: Absolutely. This is so powerful. And absolutely, so healing and so wonderful. I mentioned earlier about the forgiveness diet that you mentioned, yes, talk to us about that.

IV: That is also a tool that comes out of *A Course in Miracles*. And it's based on scripture of the Bible, where it says, "When the man asked the Christ, how many times should I forgive somebody for doing the same thing? And he said, for each offense would give them 70 times seven." And what the *Course in Miracles* did was created what's called the forgiveness diet, where for seven days, you write 35 statements in the morning, and 35 statements at night of forgiveness. So in the morning, you would write I forgive bla bla bla bla, 35 times, and then the evening you write it again, 35 times. So that's 70 times for the day. But you do it for seven consecutive days. If you miss a day, you have to start all over. Which I think is a real good way to do it. Because you need to make a commitment to yourself to the process. And if you miss a day, that says something. It has taken me as much as a month to do seven consecutive days of the forgiveness diet, because of the resistance in my consciousness. I didn't want to do it, you know? I wanted that person to pay. I wanted them to suffer. I didn't want them off the hook, you know? And I had to acknowledge that. And then I had to forgive myself for wanting to punish that person. I had to forgive myself for wanting them to suffer like I thought I had suffered. I do that in the forgiveness diet too.

BA: Yes, yes. Such a powerful tool. In a few minutes we need to go to questions. But let me ask you one thing before we go, how do you begin the conversation with someone who has angered, shamed, disappointed you?

IV: What's the point of having the conversation with them? You have to be real clear in your intention. And that's a real sticky point. Because so many of us think that if we tell the person that somehow or another, we'll feel better. But what I would say is: first have that conversation with yourself, and also have that conversation with that person in your spirit. Now you can do that on paper, you can do that with visualization, you can do that with an empty chair, have that conversation with the person. And be very clear that the purpose of the intention of the conversation is for your healing, not to get their agreement, not to get anything from them. Because you can never judge your clarity based on someone else's response. And I've heard many, many stories where people have confronted their abuser or they abandoned her or then neglect her. And the person acted like it never happened. Yeah, they had no recollection of it. That means that we all experienced differently. You know, I raised three children, and each of them are so incredibly different. I frequently say to myself, that I give them all the same grits. One pot, one stove, three different experiences, right?

BA: Absolutely.

IV: I'll have that conversation with that person. Like I said, either on paper, write what you would say, write what you think they would say, what you want them to say, have that conversation in a visualization, have that conversation with an empty chair, because it's not about them. It's about you, about you. And you really can't change anybody. You can only change yourself, Right? I've also heard stories of people who've held anger and resentment towards someone for years and years and out of the blue, that person will come to you and say, I need you to forgive me. When that happens, you know the healing has occurred.

BA: Yeah, that's pretty incredible. That is pretty incredible. Thank you so much for that.

Dorothy Roberts on Reproductive Justice

Dorothy Roberts is currently the George A. Weiss University Professor of Law and Sociology, and the Raymond Pace and Sadie Tanner Mossell Alexander Professor of Civil Rights at the University of Pennsylvania Law School. She has a joint appointment in the Departments of Africana Studies and Sociology, and she is the founding Director of the Penn Program on Race, Science and Society in the Center for Africana Studies. She is an author and an expert on the interplay of gender, race, and class in legal issues concerning reproduction, bioethics, and child welfare. This interview was broadcast on March 13, 2010.

• • •

Thandisizwe Chimurenga: According to the March 2, 2010 *Los Angeles Times*, anti-abortion activists see a racial conspiracy. It was a news article talking about the appearance of several billboards throughout metropolitan Atlanta, Georgia, a joint effort of the Georgia Right to Life campaign and the pro-adoption, pro-abstinence Radiance Foundation. This campaign says it's calling attention to the fact that Black women have a disproportionately high number of abortions. The billboards feature the face of a Black baby and the claim that "Black children are an endangered species." One well-known Black anti-abortion activist, the Reverend Clenard Childress of New Jersey, says that the most dangerous place for a Black child is the womb.

On the line with me now to discuss this latest phenomenon in what is known as the war for Black women's bodies, the war over reproductive rights and women of color, is Professor Dorothy Roberts. Professor Roberts is Professor of Law at Northwestern University in Chicago. She's the author of *Killing the Black Body: Race, Reproduction, and the Meaning of Liberty*, and also *Shattered Bonds: The Color of Child Welfare*. She's going to be speaking later on today at UCLA at a conference called by the Critical Race Studies program, a conference on intersectionality headed up by Kimberlé Crenshaw. Thank you so much, Professor Roberts, for taking the time to speak with us today.

Dorothy Roberts: Thank you. Thanks for inviting me.

TC: Professor Roberts, I greatly enjoyed, and was troubled by at the same time, your book *Killing the Black Body* when it first came out, speaking upon what is the actual meaning of liberty in terms of Black women and their bodies. This latest campaign in Atlanta, Georgia, these billboards that are being promoted by right-to-life, Pro-Life, pro-adoption, pro-abstinence organizations, some not even based in Atlanta but based in other parts of the country, that are targeting Black women stating that Black women disproportionately have abortions. This latest campaign, which is probably not financed by any organizations in Atlanta, Georgia, these billboards state that Black children are an endangered species, that abortion in the Black community is tantamount to genocide. From your perspective, what do you say about something like that?

DR: I think that these activists are twisting the history of population control policies that have targeted Black women in an attempt to devalue our childbearing and our reproductive decision-making, but they're twisting it in a way that is only blaming Black women for harm to Black children, and only going to restrict even more Black women's ability to control their own reproduction and their own bodies.

It's true that Black women have a higher rate of abortion, and it's true that there have been campaigns in the past to limit and control Black women's childbearing decisions and devalue our decisions to have children, but a Black woman seeking abortion services should not be the target of our concern. Those campaigns in the past were campaigns seeking to keep Black women from making decisions to have children.

There's a long history of that in the United States, which I detail in my book, but those campaigns were spreading the message that the reason for Black people's problems was that Black women were having too many children. It seems to me that this new campaign putting up the billboards is really doing a very similar thing because it's blaming Black women's reproductive decisions for problems in the Black community. So when this minister says the most dangerous place for a Black child is the womb, he sounds very much like sterilization abuse promoters, who promoted population control policies that punished Black women, tried to coerce them into having sterilizations on a very similar theory. That they were harming children just by having them because they were such irresponsible childbearers. That message is just being replicated in the message of these billboards. They're putting the blame in the wrong place.

The problems of Black children are not because of the reproductive decisions of Black women. We should be given more services, making available more services to Black women, so they can have greater control over their reproductive decision-making. We should be supporting policies that seek to improve the living conditions of Black mothers and their children. That's the way to reduce the number of abortions in the Black community, not by blaming mothers because they are seeking access to health care services. It focuses the blame in the wrong place, and it continues to victimize Black women as if we are the cause of social problems in this country that face Black children.

It's true that Black children are endangered, but not because of their mothers. They're endangered because of the racist practices that continue to exist in this country, and the huge amount of inequality in terms of class, race, and gender in this country. Not because Black women are seeking to have control over their own bodies.

TC: Let me ask you this. There are those who feel that based upon the statistics, over 18 million Black babies have been aborted since Roe v. Wade[1] was decided in the early 1970s. "Over 18 million Black babies aborted. Had those babies been born, there would be approximately 59 million Black folks in the United States of America. As opposed to 12 percent or 13 percent of the U.S. population, we would be approximately 20 percent

---

1 Roe v. Wade is a landmark U.S. Supreme Court case that was decided in 1973. The case addressed the issue of a woman's right to have an abortion, specifically in the first trimester of pregnancy. In a 7-2 decision, the Supreme Court held that a woman has a constitutional right to choose to have an abortion during the early stages of pregnancy. The decision remains one of the most controversial and divisive in American legal and political history.

of the population. Our numbers would be much greater. i.e., our bargaining position of power in the U.S. would be much greater had these babies not been aborted." What do you say to something like that?

DR: I would say what we have to decide is the strategy for improving the conditions of Black people in America and getting equality in this country, the struggle for equality, should it be based on increasing the numbers of babies born? If that's the case, then we would have a strategy encouraging Black women to bear more children. In this case, where the strategy is going to not only depend on encouraging Black women to have more babies but also denying them the right to terminate a pregnancy, if that's what they want to do, then you have the goal of increasing the numbers of Black people in this country on the backs of Black women. You're saying we have to restrict their right to make their own reproductive decisions in order to further the strategy of increasing the numbers of babies born.

In my opinion, the strategy should be about a struggle for increased equality and the end of white privilege and racist oppression in this country. It shouldn't be a strategy of just increasing the numbers. You can have a country with a majority of Black people. Look at South Africa, and there still is oppression, racist oppression, in the country. To me, it's not about the numbers. It's about what is our strategy for political equality. A strategy that is based on denying Black women a legal right that they have, and a human right that they have, is a bad strategy. Not only that, even more deeply than that it is a strategy that is going to blame Black women for the very unequal conditions that we have. It focuses on the wrong people. It doesn't make sense to have a social movement for equality that has folk targeting Black women as the problem. That, to me, is a completely flawed, feudal, and doomed to fail strategy.

TC: Wouldn't you say that the overall collective good of however many, 30 million, 40 million, 60 million Black people, is more important than one individual Black woman's right to choose? Wouldn't you say that?

DR: I wouldn't frame it that way, as an individual woman's right to choose versus the collective good. I would frame it as "what is the best way to further the equal human rights of Black people in this country?" I'm not saying that we shouldn't do anything about the high rates of abortion. I just think this is the wrong way to do it. I would say yes, I'm concerned about the high rates of abortion, but the way to address it is by addressing the social conditions that lead to those high rates of abortion. There is no evidence that the reason why so many Black women are getting abortions is because they're being pressured by abortion providers to get them. They may be pressured by social conditions to get them.

Whenever you have a high rate of abortion, you have to ask why are so many women who are terminating their pregnancies, why do they have unwanted pregnancies? That's the question I would want to get to. I'm not at all saying this isn't a problem. I just think that targeting Black women as the reason for the problem is the wrong way to go about it, and it focuses on the Black womb, a Black mother's womb, as a dangerous place. I think that's a dangerous message to send out.

TC: I think it is true that a Black womb is a dangerous place, but not because of these people putting up billboards in Atlanta. I think that when you look at the rates of domestic violence, the rates of violence in general, the stress that Black women are under, and when you look at the fact that incarceration is increasing, I'd say definitely the Black womb is a dangerous place to be, but it has nothing to do with the factor of abortion. That's just my humble opinion.

DR: I agree with you. And that is in line with what I'm saying, that we have to look at what are the conditions that Black people are living under in the United States. That, number one, it threatens Black children, and number two it's creating these high rates of abortion. It's not because there's something inherently dangerous about a Black woman's womb or that it's the Black woman herself and her decisions that are making it dangerous. What makes it dangerous are the unhealthy conditions, including mass incarceration, including higher rates of poverty, including the higher rates of toxins in our neighborhoods.

TC: It's always amazing to me how Pro-Life and these other organizations, they never really seem to be concerned with the conditions that these Black babies will have to grow up in. They just want them to be born, and after that, we can't find them no more. I've always been amazed by that.

DR: If people are concerned about Black children, they should be addressing the high rates of incarceration of Black men and women. They should be addressing the poor health care that's available to Black men and women, and children. They should be addressing the poor quality schools in Black neighborhoods. They should be addressing the toxins in the environment that Black people are living in. They should be addressing, in general, the racist assaults on Black people, both physical and mental, that go on. That we haven't even started to measure what impact that has on Black children in the womb.

There are so many other places to start rather than attacking these reproductive decisions of Black women. That's not the problem. That myth that the problem lies in Black women's decisions about their wombs, that myth is the same myth that has supported sterilization abuse of Black women. It's an extremely dangerous myth because it takes attention away from all of the systemic racism that still exists in America and focuses attention on the very people who are suffering from those institutions.

TC: Thank you so much, Professor Roberts, for speaking with us today. We appreciate you so much.

DR: Oh, thank you. Thanks for talking with me.

Nicole Sconiers on Black Women and Anxiety

Nicole D. Sconiers is an author and screenwriter who blends horror, sci-fi and humor in stories centering complex Black heroines. She is the author of Escape from Beckyville: Tales of Race, Hair and Rage, *a speculative fiction short-story collection and her work has been taught at colleges and universities around the country and published in numerous publications. This interview was broadcast on January 28, 2010.*

• • •

Thandisizwe Chimurenga: You're listening to *Some of Us Are Brave: A Black Woman's Radio Program* here on KPFK. My name is Thandisizwe Chimurenga and I'm speaking with Nicole Sconiers. She's the author of *California Schemin: The Black Woman's Guide to Surviving in LA* which, I'm sure I need to look at because I need a refresher course. And her latest project is the Dysfunctional Diva project. It's a book of personal essays from Black women who suffer from anxiety, bipolar disorder, and or body dysmorphia. That's a big word. Welcome to the show. Nicole.

Nicole Sconiers: Thank you, Thandi, for having me.

TC: Thank you for coming on. The first thing I would say when I see Dysfunctional Diva? Okay, on the one hand, you're dysfunctional, but you're still a diva? Tell me about this.

NS: Well, Dysfunctional Diva is a term that I coined about eight or nine years ago in my book *California Schemin'*. And at the time, it was a funny way of talking about Black women who, "she rocks Versace, but she can't spell it. She's an actress. She drives a Benz but she sleeps on a futon." But when I was diagnosed with anxiety in 2001, I reclaimed that title Dysfunctional Diva, I guess, to take the stigma away from having a mental health disorder. And so being a Dysfunctional Diva is saying, "I have anxiety. I have a mental health challenge, but I'm still fly."

TC: So being anxious, is that when we talk about having anxiety, are we saying that being anxious is a mental health disorder?

NS: That's what I was diagnosed as. And it goes deeper than just feeling nervous. For me, it was like a free floating feeling of dread. I was driving myself to the emergency room every week thinking I was having a heart attack. I had chest pain, heart palpitations, and I was reluctant to seek treatment. I just thought it was stress. And it was something – if I ate healthier if I exercise, I could overcome it. But that's not what happened. That is not what happened. I eventually had to take anti-anxiety as well as antidepressant medication.

TC: And body dysmorphia? What in the world is that?

NS: Body dysmorphia is a condition where an individual has a distorted image of their body. For instance, they may think that they're ugly, their lips are too big. I've talked to women who have pulled out their hair. Just trying to fit a certain standard. So to me, I want to speak to women who are uncomfortable with their bodies. And I want to know why, I want to know about the cultural stigmas attached to that.

TC: And bipolar is something we hear a lot about, but probably what we're hearing is maybe 50 percent or more misinformation. When you talk about bipolar disorder, what are you talking about?

NS: I'm talking about extreme mood swings. I know several people who have these high periods where they're energized and they can take on any task. And then they have the extreme lows where they're depressed and questioning their self-worth. To me, it's an extreme high and low of personality.

TC: This project, the Dysfunctional Diva project you're working on now? When did you get the idea for a book of personal essays?

NS: Dysfunctional Diva was a project that I started working on for grad school. And as I decided what my focus was going to be, I started questioning:

I had not talked about anxiety or other mental health challenges in a broader forum before I blogged about my own anxiety attacks, but I had not done so including the stories of other Black women who suffer from mental health challenges. And as you know, Black women are socialized to be strong, are socialized to be the backbone of our community and of our family. And so when we have the blues, and we can't get out of bed, and we can't stop crying, we don't speak out about our pain. And so what I want to accomplish with the Dysfunctional Diva project is, you know, bell hooks[1] says that healing occurs when we name our pain. And when we name our disorders, and we seek healing, and that's what I want to do with this project, to have a movement of Black women speaking out naming their pain and saying, "I'm not going to suffer in silence."

TC: Okay, since you've come up with this project, and now you are soliciting essays, you're asking people to submit for this project. Have you found that it is a lot? Is it a lot of Black women? Who are out there having these types of challenges? Because when I think of the term anxiety, I'd never really thought of that as a mental disorder. So what has been your experience? In terms of bringing this Dysfunctional Diva project to fruition? Have you come across a lot of sistas?

NS: I've spoken to grandmothers, I've spoken to students, women in the military, and these are powerful women, and you would never know that they suffered from anxiety or other types of mental health challenges, and maybe twenty to thirty women that I've talked to have suffered from some type of mental health disorder. And the common issue that I find is that they're embarrassed because they have to go to therapy, they're embarrassed because they have to take medication, it makes them feel weak somehow to say, "I can't stop crying, or I don't know why I have the blues all of a sudden, I don't know why I feel so sad." I think that the statistics for Black women who suffer from anxiety and mental health disorders are underreported. And I think it's because we don't name our pain, because we would rather say "I'm supposed to be strong, I'm supposed to deal with it," that we suffer in silence.

---

1 Gloria Jean Watkins (1952-2021), better known by her pen name bell hooks, was an American author, theorist, educator, and social critic who was a Distinguished Professor in Residence at Berea College. She is best known for her writings on race, feminism, and class.

TC: Okay, let me approach it from this angle. And I understand about the whole "the Black woman is strong. She's the backbone." I got you on that. And I also got the part about, "Well, I'm supposed to be strong, therefore, I can't really let people know that I need help." I got you on that. But what about this? What about for example, I did not know or even see-think-view anxiety as a mental disorder. When we talk about mental illness, there's clinical definitions, and then there's what I call "Black folks' common wisdom." For example, if you ask Jeffrey Dahmer,[2] I always use Jeffrey Dahmer, because he's a classic example. Jeffrey Dahmer was found to be sane for what he did. Now, if you go up to any Black person in America, on any street corner at any time, day and night and ask them was Jeffrey Dahmer crazy? They gonna say yes. And they're gonna use an expletive.

NS: Yes.

TS: So you have a clinical medical definition. And then you have quote, unquote, "common wisdom." So now in terms of common wisdom, you know, we might think, "Oh, she'll be all right. After a while, you know? She just need some space. So she just need this or that or what have you." It's really beyond that. Is that what you're saying? Are we at a point now, where it is just so beyond that?

NS: It's out of control. I can give you a quick example from my own life. I was at the movie theater with a friend. Twenty minutes into the picture, I had heart palpitations, chest pains and I said, "I'm having a heart attack. I'm going to the hospital." He took me to the emergency room. And by that time my anxiety attack peaked. But it was so strong, it was just a feeling of terror, like I was losing my mind. And I said, "I have got to get out of here." And my friend had the same perspective that you do. And he said, "You know, everybody gets anxious, sometimes everybody gets nervous," and he put my hand on his pulse. And he wanted me to see, see this is nervous. But he didn't understand that it was just a terror. It's was a terror that I lived with every day, like, "I'm gonna die, I'm afraid of crowds." It's so much more extreme than oh, you know, "Suck it up, you're having a bad day, you're depressed," it's so much more when you're driving to the

---

2 Jeffrey Dahmer (1960-1994) was an American serial killer who killed 17 men and boys between 1978 and 1991. Many of his later murders involved necrophilia and cannibalism Although diagnosed with various psychiatric disorders, Dahmer was found to be legally sane at his trial. He was sentenced to 15 terms of life imprisonment in 1992. In 1994, Dahmer was beaten to death by another inmate in a Wisconsin prison.

emergency room every Thursday at two o'clock in the morning, because you think you're going to die. That's a little bit extra.

TC: That's a bit much. Have you come across in any of your discussions and your research and your experiences, any type of indicator as to why this may be happening to so many Black women at this time?

NS: Because the majority of Black women that I have spoken to live in LA, I attribute it to this highly stressful lifestyle, you know, trying to get this audition or get this role or get this part and a lot of the women that I talked to were in the entertainment industry.

TC: Ohhhh so all the Black actresses crazy ...

[Laughter]

NS: I didn't say it – you didn't hear that from me. But then women, I'm just –

TC: Well – you might've heard it from Thandi – I'm just playin', I'm just playin' sistas! My sistas! I'm just playin'!

[Laughter]

NS: But then when I have spoken to grandmothers, and I've spoken to students and women in the military, I think it's because we've internalized so much stress. And we don't have techniques to decompress and to de-stress. And so we feel that we can't speak out when we do have this pain, like bell hooks says we can't we don't name our pain. We just allow it to build up and build up and build up. And for me, it was a stressful job. I wasn't eating right. I wasn't taking "me" time. And one day it just exploded and I found myself at the emergency room.

TC: So for people who may want to share their personal stories for the Dysfunctional Diva project, how can they do that?

NS: They can go to my website. I have a call for submissions there. I also have resources in case you do have any type of mental health challenges like the California Black Woman's Health Project, and other links on my website. So please come check me out. And if you can also send me an email to dysfunctionaldivaproject@gmail.com

TC: Nicole Sconiers, thank you so much for coming down and speaking with us today on *Some Of Us Are Brave*.

NS: Thank you Thandi for having me.

PaSean Wilson: Black Women and Fibroids

PaSean Wilson is a Brooklyn-born, Los Angeles-based actress, singer, documentary maker, vegan baker and the creator of MamaAunties Vegan Goodies. This interview was broadcast on January 28, 2010.

• • •

Thandisizwe Chimurenga: You're listening to *Some Of Us Are Brave: a Black Woman's Radio Program* here on KPFK. My name is Thandisizwe Chimurenga and January is Cervical Health Awareness Month. We couldn't let the month get up out of here without mentioning something about fibroids[1] and Black women. My guest now is sister PaSean Wilson. She's an actor and a filmmaker, currently she's working on a ninety-minute feature-length documentary called *The Stranger Within: Fibroid Stories*. It's a documentary film about unnecessary hysterectomies for fibroid tumors. Pasean Wilson, thank you so much for being on *Some Of Us Are Brave* today.

PaS ean Wilson: Thank you so much for having me. I'm excited!

TC: We're excited to have you here to talk about this subject, because this is a subject that many Black women know very well. I know I know it well. The stranger within. And when I saw that title, I was like, "Whoa, haven't I heard this before? And then you started talking about fibroids I said, "Okay, okay."

---

1 Uterine fibroids are benign smooth muscle tumors of the uterus. Between 20% to 80% of women develop fibroids by the age of 50.

PW: Yeah.

TC: Why this film?

PW: I am a Black woman who was diagnosed with fibroid tumors. And I never thought that I would be one of the Black women diagnosed with fibroid tumors. I, you know, I prided myself on exercising to keep my estrogen level down. And I was a vegan, vegetarian, very conscientious about how I ate. I was on a spiritual path. So I was like, "Okay, that's gonna happen to them *other* sisters ... that ain't happenin' to me ... "

TC: 'Cause you got it all together.

PW: I got it together. And I went to my doctor, and she said, "Oh, you have fibroids." I said "Huh, what?!" And she said, "Yeah, but they're small, and we'll just watch them." I was like, okay. So I went to another doctor, because that doctor stopped taking my insurance and she said, "You have fibroids. You're gonna need a hysterectomy." And ... "Really?" She's like, "Yeah, I'm gonna refer you to another doctor. But she's gonna tell you the same thing." Went to another doctor ...

TC: Well, hold on. Before we get to this third doctor, what happened to "We're gonna watch them" to "We need to take all your stuff?"

PW: Well, it depends on the doctor that you go to. That's the unfortunate part. If you're fortunate, you will go to a doctor who will say let's watch 'em. Or let's try something less invasive.

TC: I mean, had you been having issues, had you been having pain?

PW: By the second doctor, I started having issues. I started having really heavy periods, clots the size of my hand, really bad cramps. And so when she said that I needed a hysterectomy, I was flabbergasted. And so she, you know, was telling me "Don't get mad at the messenger," you know, "Any doctor will tell you the same," and she started really getting angry about the fact that I wasn't reacting. 'Cause I laughed at her, I was like, "Ha, that's not happening." I said "So how would you cut me?" And she told me how she was going to do this, you know, this scar down my belly. And I just knew that was not even an option for me. But I went to my car, and I'm gonna tell you, I cried. I wasn't gonna give her the satisfaction of seeing me cry. But I cried about it.

TC: What age did this occur?

PW: I was forty, but that didn't matter. You know, I came here with my uterus, and I'd like to leave with it unless it's cancer or something like that. So I started exploring alternative treatments. I did a number of the top name holistic doctors' programs to the tee. You know, the non-hybrid diet where you can't eat anything that's a hybrid, which leaves maybe five or six items, I'm exaggerating a little bit, but not that much. Down, went down to 95 pounds, always fasting and gotta fast. "You got to fast you got to fast you got to fast. It's the mucus, you got to melt the mucus, you got to do this, you got to do that." Did all of those programs...

TC: Ninety-five pounds ... and ninety of them was fibroids.

PW: Really. And so finally, when none of these programs worked, and the herbs and all of that stuff, I ran into someone who told me about a doctor who did a surgery called a myomectomy, which is where they take the fibroids out, they repair the uterus and you can still go on and have children if you'd like.

TC: Good Lord that sounds like a lot of work.

PW: It's a lot of work. And that's why doctors are telling women to do hysterectomies because if a doctor doesn't have the skill to do that type of intricate operation, they'll just tell you you need a hysterectomy. They won't say "Oh, I only do hysterectomies, but try this doctor around the corner. He does something else where it would preserve your uterus." They won't say that. They'll say "Oh no, you have to have a hysterectomy." "Doctor, do I have to? You have to," instead of just saying "That's what I do," and it takes a very skilled doctor to do myomectomies.

TC: Because if you have to have it and they tell you that every other doctor is going to tell you the same thing, why would you look? Why would you think, right? Why would you go elsewhere? Just sign your name on the line and get it over with.

PW: I've interviewed women in their thirties who were given hysterectomies. And I asked them why, and they said "I didn't know of any other option. I trusted my doctor, its the doctor I've had ever since I was a teenager. And he said I had to have a hysterectomy. And I didn't do any research." And that's why I'm doing the documentary. Because some women are not going to do the research, you know? So if there's a documentary out there that lets women know of all of the options, then, you know, hopefully more women will be able to preserve their uterus.

TC: Now you have a trailer of the film available on YouTube. Is that correct?

PW: Yes.

TC: I'm not sure if it's actually in the trailer on YouTube or if it's a part of the film, but you say you have audiences that are shown what an actual fibroid looks like?

PW: Yes. Dr. Stanley West wrote this book called the *Hysterectomy Hoax*, a wonderful, wonderful brother. He's been doing myomectomies for thirty-five, thirty-eight years. And I read his book and he had his phone number at the bottom of the book. I called the number and left him a message telling him my fibroid story, he called me back and said, "Sister, how can I help you? Whatever you need, if you'd like to interview my patients, if you'd like to film me doing a myomectomy, whatever you need, I want to help you do this. I can't believe that no one has done a documentary about this in all of these years, and then all of these women are being given hysterectomies." And so he let me film him doing a myomectomy and he was doing an "impossible" myomectomy because the woman he was operating on had been told by several doctors, "It's impossible for you to have a myomectomy, you have to have a hysterectomy." So when he finished his surgery, he looked in the camera he said, "I just performed another 'impossible' myomectomy."

And it's really sad. It really, it upsets me so much. I talked to women in their twenties even. I interviewed two women who were told while they were in their twenties that they had to have a hysterectomy. Fortunately, they didn't listen, they ended up having a myomectomy and each of them have two kids apiece now.

TC: Now your research, these interviews that you've been conducting. They've been all across the U.S.?

PW: Across the U.S. In Philly I interviewed sister Sonia Sonia Sanchez, the poet, because she had fibroids. Wonderful, wonderful interview subject. Philly, California, Atlanta. You know, wherever I hear an interesting story, that's where I go.

TC: I was told several years ago that Mississippi was a dangerous place for women's uteruses.

PW: Ohhh ... forget it. Forget it. The south?

TC: If you're traveling through Mississippi hold on to your uterus.

PW: The South? Yeah, it's like a rite of passage. Its like, "Yeah I'm 40 years old, it's almost time for me to have 'the surgery'." You know, because their mothers had it. The grandmothers had it. And you know, it's just like, they know they're going to have it.

TC: It's a done deal.

PW: They're not being presented with the options. It's criminal. That's the thing. Even if you believe strongly that the woman should have a hysterectomy at least tell her the options so that she can decide, because their thing is it's a band-aid. As long as a woman is over-producing estrogen, which is making these fibroids grow, if you take the fibroids out, but don't get rid of the estrogen problem, they can come back. So they're saying, "You know what, that's a band-aid cure, take the uterus out, you never have to worry about getting fibroids again." Let me make that decision whether I want a cure or a band-aid.

TC: It would seem to me that the cure would be to stop over-producing estrogen!

PW: They're not even trying to investigate that because they'd be out of business, no more surgeries! Please. My husband works for health insurance companies so it's okay if I say this – there's an incentive for the doctors to do hysterectomies because once the uterus is out, you're done with the woman. But if you do a myomectomy, shoot, five or six more years, that insurance company got to pay for another surgery, they're not trying to have that.

TC: And that's what I was going to ask you, that's part of what the hoax is isn't it? It's all about the dollars, all about the money.

PW: It's all about the dollars, but even more so than that, because I thought at first I thought it was a "Ooo a Black woman thing ... theys tryna, you know, sterilize us!" You know? Might be some of that to it. But I've interviewed a bunch of Caucasian women, some of whose husbands are doctors, and they gave them hysterectomies for fibroids, because that whole mentality of "cure," cure, that, you know, that God complex "I got to cure you." And then they tried to throw in the cancer, the "C" word. They said that to me too. "Well your fibroids are so big it might be hiding cancer." "Well, do you have any evidence of this, blood test, anything like statistics?" Nothing. Scare tactic.

TC: Scare tactic. Fascinating, but it also makes me so angry.

PW: Yeah.

TC: You know, I was in a good mood when I came here. But girl you done got me worked up right now.

PW: You know, that's why one doctor I talked to, a holistic doctor, her theories why Jewish women are having fibroids almost as much as African-American women, is that same feeling of oppression and that stuffing of rage. Melanin thing, too. We get the little nappy hair we got the melanin going on. So um, who knows what it is, but I want to start dialoguing and some of the theories are gonna be crazy. I've heard its because sisters and Jewish women get relaxers and the chemicals pool "down there." I've heard that theory, I've heard it's mucus, hardened mucus. I've heard it. I've heard all kinds of theories.

TC: Okay, well, my hair is not relaxed [Laughter]

PW: Neither is mine

TC: Neither is yours. I haven't done the "fast" thing to the extent you did it, probably never will do it that to that extent, but no. Okay. How can we get more information on *The Stranger Within: Fibroid Stories* and PaSean Wilson?

PW: Well, you can always Facebook me. I'm on Facebook for PaSean Wilson.

TC: PaSean Wilson, thank you so much for being on *Some Of Us Are Brave* today.

PW: Thank you!

The March for Women's Lives

The March for Women's Lives was held on April 25, 2004, in Washington, DC. One of the largest demonstrations of its time with well over 1 million participants, the March was held in support of reproductive freedom and justice for women. Pacifica Radio's five station network broadcast the event live from the National Mall. The following comments aired on Some of Us Are Brave. Exact date unknown.

• • •

Thandisizwe Chimurenga: Whoopi Goldberg is the emcee for the March for Women's Lives, one of the MCs, and in her opening address, she held up a clothes hanger, saying to the crowd "Remember this? This is what it was like 30 years ago. We're not going back to this. Never again." I was standing next to a Muslimah (Muslim woman) who said she had firsthand knowledge of what it was like, before Roe v. Wade, when Whoopi was talking about that clothes hanger. I asked her to tell me more.

Unidentified Muslimah

UM: Yes, I know about it very well, because I experienced it. Personally. There was a, a woman that I was referred to. I was pregnant, about 19 years old. And I didn't want to have a child at that point in time, I was in college, and I was getting ready to move to California. And I felt that "No, I can't go through this." So, some friends recommended me to a woman and I went to her. And needless to say, I wasn't quite sure what it was that she actually stuck up inside of me. But whatever it was, it did induce the delivery or abortion of the fetus [that] was inside of me. And about a day or two later, I had hemorrhaging, a lot of hemorrhaging. And my mother wasn't even aware of what had happened. And she wasn't sure what was going on. All she knew was that she needed to get me to the hospital.

And after that experience, there were other sisters that I was talking with, who also did similar things to themselves or had someone else to do that. And, and many of them were unable to have children later on. Because I mean, obviously, it's not the way to do it. And for me, I thank God, I was able to have a child later in life, and I also have a grandchild, but just seeing that hanger at times to tell you the truth, even when I see a wire hanger now, I get a little fearful. Not that I'm going to do anything or that anyone else is going to do anything; the most I would use that for now is to probe into a toilet, okay? And that is surely not something that you want up inside of your body.

TC: When was this?

UM: That happened in the 1960s ... the late 60s in fact, so ... let me just say also that, as far as pro-choice goes, I can't say that I honestly feel that I believe in abortions at this point in my life. But I do feel that a woman, *a woman,* should have the right to be able to do what she feels is necessary for her and her body. And I don't want any man or any woman to say that they are the ones who are going to determine through some law, some state law, that they are the ones who will say "No, you can't do this." I mean, and if it's that important, I would like to see them being a lot more active, a lot more proactive with our healthcare situation. Our healthcare is deplorable in this country. To think that this is supposed to be one of the richest countries, and their biggest issue is about abortion, yes or no. When there are people dying from high blood pressure, diabetes, cancer, HIV, and on and on and on. Our children, they can't get the proper health care that they need. Our elderly. Myself, I'm a professional woman and I don't have health insurance. I resent the fact that the people in our Congress, our legislators seem to feel that this is the only issue that they need to sit on and deal with every. Every year! I'm tired of it. Thank you.

TC: Where are you from?

UM: Today? Today I'm from the DC area.

TC: May I ask your age?

UM: I'm over 50.

TC: One last question. You said that you are Muslim?

UM: Yes I am.

TC: But even though you are Muslim, you still believe that a woman should have choice?

UM: This is, I really, I may have a lot of people that would come out against me saying something like this, but women do have choices. Even in Islam, they have a choice. They will have to deal with it with Allah, and on Judgement Day, but and I'm not, again, I am not advocating abortion, but I am advocating choice. And the choice has to do with free will. And you have to make your own decision. And you have to be the one who has to live with that. But I don't appreciate and don't like having someone else sitting in judgment of my life and my body.

Thank you.

Luz Rodriguez

LR: I'm the co-founder of SisterSong: Women of Color Reproductive Health Collective.

TC: What is SisterSong?

LR: SisterSong is a collective of women of color organizations and individuals who are networking together throughout the country to support women of color, in any and all of their human rights, including reproductive health and access to health and any of the rights that pertain to being a woman in this country and the world.

TC: So it's reproductive health and other issues?

LR: Well, reproductive health has, the time has come for people to understand that reproductive health is a human rights issue. And if a woman doesn't have her full, human rights, reproductive health is one of the consequences. But there are other consequences, particularly with women of color that are threatening women's wellbeing. So those of us who have been in the reproductive health movement realize that the framework needs to broaden the realities of what women of color face, so it's really human rights issues. Bottom line.

TC: You are a Latina woman?

LR: Yes, I am. I'm Puerto Rican.

TC: We all know what the perception is of the reproductive rights movement, of the women's movement … It's seen as a white woman's issue. How long have you been involved in this work?

LR: I became involved as a young college girl when I started finding out that Puerto Rican women on the island had been used as guinea pigs for the contraceptive pill. This was, I believe back in the, I really can't say right now I don't recall. But I believe back in the early 1950s, when the contraceptive pill was being tested, Puerto Rican women on the island were seen as appropriate specimens to test the pill. And these women were given 10 times the normal dose that's allowed now. And they were being tested without informed consent. There are also reports of sterilization abuses, where women were sterilized without informed consent on the island. And what I learned is that reproductive and contraceptive technologies were being tested and implemented as a population control issue when it comes to people of color. The government's interested in population control, and that's what reproductive technologies and issues were about with respect to the powers that be. So, when you include women of color issues, that's why it becomes a human rights issue and a racial justice issue and an equality issue beyond a woman's issue.

TC: Thank you.

LR: You're welcome.

Mabel Thomas

MT: 'Able' Mabel Thomas, State Representative from Atlanta, Georgia. I feel that it really is a march to save women lives. I think that women have been pushed back, there has been an open war against women. From every policy you can look at, from the federal government down to our state legislature. You see policy to trying to turn the clock back. So if women don't take a stand, we will be pushed further back and generations behind us will suffer. So really it is me taking a stand for my own life and taking a stand for all the young people and women that will come behind me.

TC: Many people have, many of the women of color who have come here today, have said that this is an issue of human rights. Do you feel that way?

MT: It's ... [inaudible] human rights and economic justice. The real deal is that we need economic policies that make sure that we actually get not only get equal pay for equal work, but we actually all have access to the opportunities for business ownership, to make sure that we have jobs that are high-paying jobs so that we can make a livable wage. It's a human rights issue, because we're talking about not only just freedom of choice, but we're talking about freedom to make decisions about our lives, and to live productive lives and really be a part of what we call the American Dream. Thank you.

Wanda Sykes

WS: I'm Wanda Sykes. I'm here because I believe in the cause. And this administration has just gotten out of hand and they are like, I think after you know, after they finish up with Iraq, we're next. I mean, women, we're being attacked. And we got to tell them to keep their grubby mitts off our bodies. You know, I bet you if Halliburton[1] had a contract for abortion clinics, they'd be mandatory, they'd be making us all get abortions. Dick Cheney,[2] all of them, they'd be knocking women up left and right just to make them go to Halliburton to get their abortion. So, I'm sick of them. I'm sick of them. And we all need to get out there. Vote November, vote, get these monkeys out of office. They're evil, get 'em out.

TC: [Laughing]

I was gonna ask you, as a comedian, why are you here today? I mean, is this, this doesn't seem like a comedian's sphere ... but you characteristically [Laughing]

WS: Oh I'ma find some funny in it. [Laughing] You know, the funny, it's about a, you know, just a cause. And you know, and that's what comics do, when we see something's wrong, we say "It's a problem going on,"ya know? It's our job to point it out, ya know? Got to expose it.

TC: Thank you very much.

WS: Thank you. Get your 'bortion! Halliburton!

[Laughter]

---

1 Halliburton Company is an American multinational corporation responsible for most of the world's hydraulic fracturing operations. In 2009, it was the world's second largest oil field service company with operations in more than 70 countries. It owns hundreds of subsidiaries, affiliates, branches, brands, and divisions worldwide. It is notable for its questionable business practices during its relationship with former Vice-President Dick Cheney.

2 Dick Cheney (born 1941) served as the vice president of the United States from 2001 to 2009 under President George W. Bush.

Dazon Dixon Diallo

DDD: I am the founder and president of SisterLove Inc., which is a women's HIV/AIDS and sexual reproductive health and rights organization in Atlanta, Georgia. And a couple other things [laughter] I also am a Professor of Women's Health in the School of Public Health at Morehouse School of Medicine and I teach in the Women's Studies program at Spelman College.

TC: See I didn't know you did all of that, then I'm not going to ask you "why are you here today?"

[Laughter]

DDD: Well see? [Laughter] And then I host and produce Sisters' Time on WRFG 89.3-FM Atlanta, a Pacifica affiliate.

TC: How did you find the time to come here today, let me ask you that?

DDD: I *made* the time to come here today. As a matter of fact, I took my scholarship, and instead of buying a plane ticket, I rented a car so that we could bring more. With SisterLove, our work has been at the intersection of HIV and sexual reproductive health and rights. And the only way to keep HIV in the conversation is to make sure that we articulate it in a way that people understand HIV as a reproductive rights issue, as an issue around choice, as an issue around women's sexual rights, sexual identity, sexual expression, and there's room to talk about that right here. So that's why we're here. Full. We also are a member of SisterSong: Women of Color Reproductive Health Collective, a national body of women who, women of color, individuals and organizations who all are working from the same agenda around women of color and our reproductive health and our reproductive health challenges with regard to justice and health care are extremely important, especially for women living with HIV. So we organized a bus to say that.

TC: So how many people did you come here with today?

DDD: I don't even really know the number. [Laughter] I know that we had a full bus of about 40-plus people. We also had a car load, we also had at least four or five people coming in on the airplane. And that's just the SisterLove part of the delegation. Georgia came in full force with about 16 buses, I believe. And we're just here, just, I don't even know but we're making up a million [Laughter]

TC: In terms of Black women and reproductive health, we have all, we have never really had a choice in terms of whether or not we wanted to reproduce. We were brought here, enslaved, and it was massa's choice for us to, who to breed with and how many children to have. And we still suffer from that legacy. Is there, in your travels, does that legacy of being based in the south, being based in Georgia, the shadow of the plantation - is it really the shadow? Is it still in effect?

DDD: Well, yeah, I mean, a conversation I was having earlier, I think, is that situations like what happened or what policies were made legal for men and other human beings to control other human beings was simply a framework that was laid for all further action. If you create an institutionalized environment that allows another human being to treat another human being with control, with ownership with less than human attributes, then of course you're gonna, it doesn't matter who you're doing it to, you're going to lay that foundation and it's going to be a part of the fabric of what we call America forever. I mean, it wasn't just Africans; Native Americans' population was controlled by the colonizers. African and African American or people born in this country, reproduction was controlled by white people who "owned" them by the law, and by legal standards. So, they already created an environment where that was acceptable to do that. Let's translate it to today: how can any adult think that it is acceptable to not give a young person all the access to sex education so they can save their own lives? That's another form of slavery. That's another form of controlling someone else's humanity. As if your humanity is the only important humanity. Well, we're all here. And anytime you think you can control me, then you're saying that I'm less than. And there's a problem there because the minute we're able to say, "Okay, now we're in control," y'all gonna have some real issues. *Real issues.*

TC: Thank you.

DDD: [Laughter] But, I'm serious. It's as basic as that. You are not going to control my body and still consider yourself a proponent of human rights. And anyone who says so is double-speaking or lying.

TC: Thank you.

DDD: Thank you very much for having me. And for all that you do.

Honorable Sheila Jackson Lee

SJL: I'm a member of Congress in the 18th Congressional District in Houston, Texas. I believe that this has to be one of the singular most important moments in America's history for women of color, for the disenfranchised, for women of America. I'm here because I believe, even though when the Constitution was written, I was two thirds of a person. I believe the constitutional concept and the Bill of Rights was written for me; the 14th amendment of equal protection under the law; and the Ninth Amendment; the right to privacy, the right to protect those rights reserved for the people. We have lost, over the last four years, many of those rights, whether it's a question of choice; whether it's a question of equal access to health care and the fight against HIV/AIDS and the acknowledgement that more African American women are dying between the ages of 25 and 44 by HIV/AIDS; whether it's childcare; whether it's the question of young men and women that come from the inner cities of America, rural America dying in Iraq, one by one, two by two. This is a statement that we want to take our country back. We are a nation of people and of laws, but the people are here to speak of the tragedy of what we are facing and the only way we can do this is by galvanizing and providing that engine of power to make a difference.

Thank you.

Bruthas on Sistas

Clayton Lebouef on Henrietta Vinton Davis

Clayton Lebouef is a theater, film and spoken word performer, as well as a playwright. Aired December 10, 2009.

• • •

Thandisizwe Chimurenga: You're listening to *Some of Us Are Brave: A Black Women's Radio Program*. My name is Thandisizwe Chimurenga and November 23 is the anniversary of the death of Henrietta Vinton Davis, an actress, journalist and cultural worker in the early half of the 20th century.

Not much is known about Henrietta Vinton Davis, but we're hoping to change that with my next guest. His name is Clayton LeBouef; he's a first rate cultural worker, an actor best known for his work on *Homicide: Life On the Street* and HBO's *The Wire*. He is a co-founder of the Henrietta Vinton Davis Foundation. Thank you so much for being on our show today. How are you doing?

Clayton Lebouef: I am feeling really good. Thank you Thandi, and I hope you are as well.

TC: Yes. I'm wonderful, wonderful. Please tell our audience how you came to know of Henrietta Vinton Davis first of all?

CLB: Yes. I was doing a play in Baltimore, Maryland when *Homicide* was just starting out. And I came across a book called *Shakespeare in Sable*. It's a book about Black Shakespearean actors by Errol Hill. And I was reading this book since I was doing either *Pericles* or *Romeo and Juliet*, I forget now.

And there was a whole chapter in the book on a lady that I had never heard of because, while I had heard of Ira Aldridge,[1] I had heard of obviously Paul Robeson[2] and other Shakespearean actors of note, Robert Hooks[3] right out there in Los Angeles. And he was in the book and others, but I had never heard of this particular woman born in Baltimore, Maryland and did most of her work in Washington DC, which is where I'm based. And after reading that chapter, first I couldn't believe I had never heard of her with all of the accomplishments that I was reading in the book. And that was my introduction to this wonderful woman.

TC: Now, in addition to being an actor of Shakespeare and other works, she was also a Garveyite[4] and utilized her cultural work, her cultural ethos or should I say Garvey's, formed her cultural ethos and her cultural work. Would that be correct?

CLB: Yes. That was a while later where she had established herself across the country as what they call an elocutionist, which is another word for someone who speaks well; an actor like you would have today, one-woman shows or one-man shows. She would travel and do monologues from Shakespeare or from different poets. And so they called her an elocutionist or a reader. It's been stated that she was the first Black woman to read Shakespeare to the public, something we still have to do some more research on, but that has been stated in a couple of the sources that myself and a brother by the name of Nnamdi Azikiwe who is the co-founder of the Henrietta Davis Memorial Foundation.

And so she established herself as a great actor. But as time went on she was never allowed into what they call the "legitimate theater circle," which is a way of saying allowed into what they call mainstream or white theater

---

1 Ira Aldridge (1807-1867) was an actor, playwright, and theatre manager, known for his portrayal of Shakespearean characters. Facing discrimination in America, he left in 1824 for England and made his debut at London's Royal Coburg Theatre. He subsequently became manager of Coventry's Theatre Royal. Aldridge is the only actor of Black-American descent honoured with a bronze plaque at the Shakespeare Memorial Theatre in Stratford-upon-Avon.

2 Paul Robeson (1898-1976) was an American singer, actor, and civil rights activist. Robeson was an outspoken advocate for civil rights and a supporter of many progressive causes, including labor rights and anti-colonialism. He faced persecution during the McCarthy era for his political beliefs and was blacklisted in the United States. Despite this, he continued to perform and speak out for his beliefs until his death in 1976.

3 Robert Hooks (1937-) is an actor, producer, and activist. He was one of the founders of the Negro Ensemble Company in New York, which is credited with the launch of the careers of many major Black artists of all disciplines. It is also known for creating a body of performance literature, providing the backbone of African-American theatrical classics.

4 See note on Marcus Garvey on page 16.

establishments. And that led her to do her own thing and she travelled to Jamaica and heard the words of Mr. Garvey. And that's when she moved in that direction of utilizing her skills as elocutionist, dramatic reader as they call them, dramatic reader/actor, and was very, very instrumental in introducing Mr. Garvey to audiences all across the country.

TC: This is not the first time I heard about the women in Garvey's sphere, in how they hooked him up.

CLB: Oh, yes.

TC: There is a book called *Seeing Red,* which talks about the military intelligence division, which was the precursor to the FBI, and they talked about the fact that, "You know we got to look out. We got to keep our eye on this Garvey because he's been meeting with a lady named Ida B. Wells." So I see also that there is a number of Black women who were instrumental in helping Garvey achieve the heights that he achieved. So can you tell us a little bit more about Pan-Africanism and the Garveyism of Henrietta Vinton Davis, especially as it relates to theater?

CLB: Yes. What she would do is open up for Garvey as he travelled, because as you know she was much older than Garvey by maybe what? She was in her mid-twenties when Garvey was born, so you see the age difference there. And when he came over from London and started the organization, people would come out to see her.

She was known through Black newspapers for her dramatic reading. She would do things like say "a little brown baby with the sparkling eyes," a poem, and then a Black doll would be on stage with her. And the Garvey movement – a very misunderstood movement in this country and we're gonna have to revisit it to get our balance – they owned a lot of businesses, hat companies, clothing, they had poets.

It is my contention as well as others that the Garvey movement actually was the Harlem Renaissance. But we must remember, when some people are lifted, when attention comes to them, that doesn't mean that there are others that aren't doing the work that were not, you know what I mean?

We have jazz artists, we have great visual artists, painters. Just because they're not famous does not mean they don't exist, and that has been a big problem in our country. So you had many people around Henrietta in the Garvey movement that she worked right along with too, doing plays. There were playwrights within the UNIA, Universal Negro Improvement Association. We call it the Garvey movement, but that again does somewhat of a disservice to the movement, because it's people like Lady Davis and other men and women who we don't know, they didn't become famous.

This is why she's very important because she is going to lead us back to men and women who were not lifted by other people and stated, "Well, these are the people who are famous." So these are the people, but we have our grandfathers, our grandmothers. So her work to answer your question, her work within the movement was not to so much get famous on the outside of anything. It's to work directly with people who were business people, who owned businesses, social, community, organizers working right within the community and used the arts not so much as an entertainment vehicle; utilizing entertainment but also using it as a social balance, because we can be entertained, you know, forever. But there's a social balance that comes with culture and entertainment. We're having fun but we're also learning a number of things. And we fell more into an entertainment side. She didn't.

As a matter of fact, she refused to go into a minstrel show that was available to her, you know, at one of the times that they – I'm not certain of right now. But I hope that kind of gives you somewhat of a clue. Working with people and theater, groups, oratory contests, poetry, recitals, small plays. She would play men, Dessalines,[5] Henri Christophe.[6] She was doing untraditional casting of herself and working within the Garvey movement, making it relevant to life rather than, "Oh, this is just something we do and we just entertain and we come out and we sing and dance." They had serious drama rather than just a lot of comedy and silliness.

TC: Now there was also the call for independent Black theater. Is that correct?

CLB: Well, it was actually happening. All across the country, we had Black people doing things. But as the history books lay out, take for example

---

5 Jean-Jacques Dessalines (1758-1806) was a leader of the Haitian revolution and the first ruler of an independent Haiti under the 1805 constitution. Dessalines was later named Emperor of Haiti as Jacques I (1804-1806) and ruled in that capacity until his assassination in 1806. He has been referred to as the father of the nation of Haiti.

6 Henri Christophe (1767-1820) was a key leader in the Haitian Revolution. Beginning with the slave uprising of 1791, he rose to power in the ranks of the Haitian revolutionary military. After Dessalines was assassinated, Christophe created a separate government, and in 1811, Christophe was proclaimed Henry I, King of Haiti. In 1820, he committed suicide.

the Harlem Renaissance. There are certain writers that we've all come to know: Langston Hughes[7] obviously, Countee Cullen[8] and others. But those were the artists that became well-known with backing from other people. But right with, inside of the Garvey Movement, take for example Mr. Garvey himself and his wife were playwrights.

We have a similar situation today. Louis Farrakhan[9] is a playwright and a world-class violinist. A lot of times we don't have that discussion and some people even till today are quite surprised when they find out that he's a playwright and he's a world-class violinist. And they come out of that tradition is the reason why I mentioned him. From the Harlem Renaissance, we know certain artists. Today we know our August Wilson.[10] But there was a John Henry Redwood,[11] so I'm jumping back and forth but it's very important. This is why I'm passionate about her because she's opening up the discussions that you and I are having now.

We can talk about the past, but make it relate to today rather than saying, "We had great writers in the Harlem Renaissance, but today we don't have writers like that." We've always had them. They've always been there. They've never gone, but just because they are not recognized and made famous by other people who recognize them as being great.

TC: Yes, sir.

CLB: We lose a lot of people that way.

TC: Yes, sir.

CLB: I was reading an article, "The Day," by Dr. Ron Daniels. And he called for what's needed as a cultural offensive. Meaning, how can culture help us get balance with our young people and others? How do we use culture/entertainment?

---

7 Langston Hughes (1902-1967) was an American poet, novelist, and playwright who is best known for his powerful and moving depictions of African-American life in the United States. Hughes was an important figure in the Harlem Renaissance, a cultural movement that emerged in the 1920s and 1930s. Hughes was also involved in the civil rights movement who used his writing to call attention to social and political issues.
8 Countee Cullen (1903-1946) was a poet, novelist, and essayist associated with the Harlem Renaissance. He was one of the most prominent African-American writers of his time and is known for his lyrical poetry, which often explored themes of race, love, and identity. He was also involved in various civil rights organizations.
9 See note on Louis Farrakhan on page 73.
10 August Wilson (1945-2005) was an acclaimed playwright. He is best known for his "Pittsburgh Cycle," a series of ten plays that explore the lives of African-Americans in the 20th century. Wilson was the recipient of numerous awards and honors for his work, including two Pulitzer Prizes for Drama and a Tony Award for Best Play.
11 John Henry Redwood (1942-2003) was author of numerous works for the American theatre and a lauded actor who appeared on Broadway in August Wilson's *The Piano Lesson* and a revival of *Guys and Dolls*.

And see that word is not used a lot. We hear entertainment, but culture sometimes – You don't hear a lot of people talk about the industry of culture. We talk about the entertainment business. This is show business. But when someone says, "Let's get into culture," then all of a sudden it's not as easy to talk about this. We're talking about culture.

Now you're going into deeper areas of how entertainment can be used to keep the people healthy. That's what culture is. And this is what her work was about.

TC: Tell us about the Henrietta Vinton Davis Memorial Foundation.

CLB: It's very new. Fairly new. I received a call one day from Nnamdi Azikiwe, a young man, researcher, writer, filmmaker, upcoming artist who had found my play, the play that I wrote on Miss Davis. It was at the Schomburg Center for Research in Harlem. He found the play there as he was doing his research.

TC: Let's back up for a minute. Just encapsulate for me, you wrote a play on Henrietta Vinton Davis. What led you to write this play?

CLB: Thank you for asking me, I'm moving kind of fast. After I read that book *Shakespeare in Sable* I began to do more research, because just like everyone who is hearing about her accomplishments I kept saying, "How did this lady slip by me?" How have I been involved in theater – and obviously you don't know everything, we all have to learn – but I had never heard anything of her, and especially since I'm based in the DC/Baltimore area.

So I started asking different people and I was coming up short with scholars, with theater people who had never heard of her. Never heard of her. Not that they had heard in little dribs and drabs maybe, but like clean slate I never heard of the woman. The more I started asking people the more interesting it got. And as I started trying to do my research I found little things. It was very little, in microfilm or microfiche of the research, Garvey papers. And I said, "I have to write. I have to write a play about this woman."

So I started doing more research, putting little notes together. And I ended up writing a play that was commissioned as I spoke to some children in an after-show discussion. I was doing some work at Center Stage again. I have a relationship with them as an actor. And they had never heard of her and they commissioned me to write the piece. And once I handed it to them, I think it was a little too heavy for what they were looking for at the time.

They were interested in the Shakespeare aspect of it, but then the Garvey aspect might have been just a little bit too progressive or nationalistic for their taste, so they didn't put the show up.

So I put a beautiful staged reading on up at the Women's Museum here in DC, and then that led to the call from Mr. Azikiwe. He was doing research just like I was. You know how it happens? Just like when you called me, you never know who is reading what.

TC: How did Nnamdi find you?

CLB: I was working in my study one day and I received a call and he introduced himself and he told me "I have found a copy of your play." At that time it was called *Shero: the Livication of Henrietta Vinton Davis*. It is now called *The Life and Breath of Henrietta Davis*. And he says, "I found it at the Schomburg Center for Research in Harlem."

And I stopped him right there. This is our first conversation. I have never met him, seen him. I said, "Well, thank you for telling me. I had no clue that a copy of my play was at the Schomburg. This was new information." So I was kind of confused as to how it got there. I came to find out later how it got there was through me doing a workshop at the National Black Theater Festival in Winston Salem, North Carolina, in the festival that they have there and I handed in a script.

So it came back to me through my discussion with him. But he had been searching for me because he was fascinated with the play. He had been doing deeper research. He had gone into some very deep research that I have yet to get to. So he reached out to me. We met, and when I sat down with this brother he began to pull out information that I have never seen in my research. And part of that information was where she was laid to rest, at Harmony Memorial National Park Cemetery with no headstone. No marker, as if this woman – And she obviously has been forgotten by so many people.

He had that kind of research as well as others. So I said, "Hey, man. Maybe you can serve as a dramaturge[12] as I continue to develop this play." The types

---

12 A dramaturge is a professional in the field of theater or film who is responsible for the research, analysis, and development of a production's dramatic and literary aspects. The role varies depending on the context, but generally involves working closely with directors, playwrights, and other members of the creative team to ensure the overall coherence and effectiveness of a performance. In essence, a dramaturge serves as a bridge between the creative vision of the playwright or director and the audience, helping to enrich the overall theatrical experience.

of information that he had, my script was in its first draft and you know how things go, they go through. So we began to meet and as we found we have mutual concerns about the theater arts, what it means, we formed this foundation called the Henrietta Vinton Davis Memorial Foundation to honor her with a headstone marker to make her known throughout the country and wherever she travels, which was overseas as well. And to utilize this beautiful angel, this beautiful ancestor to now do what Dr. Ron Daniels is talking about – a cultural movement to let our people know we have to seriously honor those who've come.

And someone says, "Well, aren't we doing that now?" Well, that's up for debate. So many, I would be wanting to say we're not doing nowhere near enough to honor. We've had wonderful people, and not only in the arts. I don't know if you've seen a piece that I was in on HBO called *Something the Lord Made* where I played opposite Mos Def[13] in a wonderful film about a Black man named Vivien Thomas[14] ...

TC: How could I forget when I introduced you! I'm so sorry for forgetting!

CLB: Oh, don't be sorry at all because you know, we bring it back, it all comes back around. These stories are fascinating that he is a man responsible for heart surgery in this country and people have never heard of them.

TC: Don't know. Never heard of them.

CLB: This is not ancient African history. The beautiful things that we learn about ancient African history have helped us immensely get balance as a people. When we read about the great civilizations, this is what has kept us going. However, right here in this country we're now at the next phase. We've learned about some ancient African history, more coming, but now it's starting to be revealed as well right here where we were physically placed as people of diaspora. Learning about inventors, learning about people who are responsible for many, many things to help all of humanity progress.

---

13 Mos Def (born 1973), also known as Yaslin Bey, is an American rapper, singer, songwriter, and actor. He was a child actor in television films, sitcoms, and theater. He has been vocal on several social and political causes, including police brutality, American exceptionalism, and the status of African Americans.

14 Vivien Thomas (1910-1985) was an American laboratory supervisor who developed a procedure used to treat blue baby syndrome (now known as cyanotic heart disease) in the 1940s. Thomas was unique in that he did not have any professional education, yet he served as supervisor of the surgical laboratories at Johns Hopkins University for 35 years.

And this foundation is beautiful because when you look at Garvey and the people around him now it's starting to come out and it's like, "We can't get stuck on one individual. We can't get stuck on just Malcolm. What about the elders that Malcolm was around?" You know how about these folk? How about Sister Mother Tynnetta,[15] a sister who was a great woman doing great work teaching people about what's happening in Mexico and the Mayan calendar. What about our own grandmothers and grandfathers that we have to take another look at when we act crazy because we can sit and watch a football game and get crazy and argue with each other on who's a better team, and those arguments lead to serious fights.

And just the way we act and hear our grandmothers and grandfathers that went through so much to put us in this position. We are gonna have to really take another look through film and through theater, which is you know one way to take a look at it. And tell these different stories; the foundation is actually leading in that direction.

TC: Clayton LeBouef; a co-founder of the Henrietta Vinton Davis Memorial Foundation, cultural worker, actor, playwright, the creator of *The Life and Breath of Henrietta Vinton Davis*, an international organizer with the Garvey movement, elocutionist, actor, revered ancestor. Thank you so much for the work that you have done to bring this ancestor to, bring her back to us, to help remind us of who she is. Thank you so much for this important work.

CLB: Well, Thandi, I have to thank you because obviously you, your research team with the radio show that honors women, it's obviously right on time. Things are happening. I received your call, found out about the work that you were doing at the station with this particular program and I think as people learn more about all of the women that will be coming forth, Henrietta, others that will be coming forth known and unknown in the work that you're doing. But your show has been a pleasure for me to meet with you and talk with you to share this information.

TC: Thank you so much for your time.

CLB: Thank you.

---

15 Tynnetta Muhammad (1941-2015) was a scientist, writer, and spiritual leader of the Nation of Islam. In the 1960s, she wrote articles and columns for the Nation of Islam newsletter *Muhammad Speaks*. She was the mother of four children of Elijah Muhammad and was regularly referred to as "Mother Tynnetta Muhammad" in the movement.

Dr. Gerald Horne on Shirley Graham Du Bois

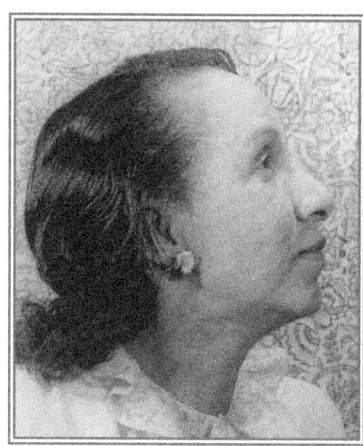

Dr. Gerald Horne holds the Moores Professorship of History and African American Studies at the University of Houston. His research has addressed issues of racism in a variety of relations involving labor, politics, civil rights, international relations and war, and film. Aired November 19, 2009

• • •

Thandisizwe Chimurenga: November 11, 1896 is the birthdate of Shirley Graham Du Bois. Most of us are familiar, or we should be familiar, with the activist and theoretical work of her husband, Dr. William Edward Burghardt Du Bois.[1] But we're not really that familiar with her work.

Shirley Graham Du Bois was an activist, scholar, artist and Pan-Africanist in her own right. I've asked Dr. Gerald Horne, Professor of History and African-American Studies at the University of Houston and also author of *Race Woman: A Biography of Shirley Graham Du Bois*, to speak with us today on this phenomenal woman. For those who have not read your book or do not know anything about this woman, tell our audience please about this remarkable woman.

Gerald Horne: She was the daughter of a pastor, but I think that why she is best known is because of her writing and her political activism. First of all, as a political activist, she was with the NAACP in the early 1940s, when it had its greatest spurt in its membership. You may recall that in 1940 the NAACP

---
1 See note on W.E.B. Du Bois on page 16.

– the National Association for the Advancement of Colored People, which was founded in 1909 by her spouse, W.E.B Du Bois – in 1940 it had a membership of about 40,000. By 1944 its membership had grown tenfold, to 400,000. It was Shirley Graham Du Bois who was basically coordinating that membership drive when this organization had such phenomenal growth in members.

It's interesting to note that the NAACP hardly has grown past that level of 400,000 to this date in 2009. So that gives you an idea of the scope of what she did during that time. But she was also a political activist in Ghana, Kwame Nkrumah's[2] Ghana. With her spouse W.E.B Du Bois, they moved to this small West African nation, where he was a pioneer in implementing Pan-African ideas in the early 1960s.

By 1963, indeed, on the eve of the March on Washington, where Martin Luther King made his famous "I Have A Dream" speech, W.E.B Du Bois was dead. But from there it's fair to say that, for whatever reason, her political activism blossomed even further. She became a close advisor to the leader of independent Ghana. I'm speaking of Kwame Nkrumah. She was in many ways the director of a project to have television, this relatively new appliance, placed in villages. Television was going to be used as a mass means of communication. But you may recall that fate intervened in the form of a military coup that took place in 1966, leading to the overthrow of Nkrumah, supposedly at the behest of the U.S. Central Intelligence Agency. Shirley Graham Du Bois was detained and barely escaped with her life.

From there, she moved to Cairo, Egypt. From Cairo she began to reinvent herself. Or I should say, she began to rededicate herself further to her writing, because she was also a very talented writer.

It was in the 1930s that she first catapulted to prominence as perhaps the leading Black woman playwright of that era. In some ways she was a complement of Zora Neale Hurston,[3] who I guess it's fair to say was the

---

2 Kwame Nkrumah (1909-1972) was a Ghanaian politician, political theorist, and revolutionary. He was the first Prime Minister (1957-1960) and President of Ghana (1960-1966), having led the Gold Coast to independence from Britain in 1957. Under Nkrumah, Ghana played a leading role in African international relations during the decolonization period. Nkrumah was deposed in 1966 and lived the rest of his life in Guinea, where he was named honorary co-president.

3 Zora Neale Hurston (1891-1960) was an American author, anthropologist, and filmmaker. She wrote four novels and more than 50 short stories, plays, and essays. Hurston's works concerned both the African-American

leading Black woman novelist of that period. But Shirley Graham Du Bois also engaged in journalism. And she also engaged in biography writing. She wrote a very interesting biography of Paul Robeson,[4] the tallest tree in our forest. She continued her journalism after repatriating to Cairo in 1966, after the overthrow of Kwame Nkrumah.

Now, that gives a thumbnail sketch of her life. But as is well known, because of her surname, Du Bois, many people know her best because sadly, her marriage to this towering intellectual W.E.B. Du Bois, who she married late in life, in the early 1950s when he was about to be put on trial because of a Cold War McCarthyite[5] frame-up. And because of her campaigning, because of her organizing skills, she played a pivotal role in assuring that the elderly Dr. Du Bois would not spend his last days in a dank prison cell.

Shirley Graham Du Bois was also a part of a very vibrant and thriving circle of left-wing Black women intellectuals. I'm speaking as well of Eslanda Robeson, who you may know as the spouse of Paul Robeson. Others know because of her pioneering work as a travel writer and as an anthropologist.

I'm also speaking of Lorraine Hansberry,[6] who was much younger than Eslanda Robeson and Shirley Graham Du Bois, but was catapulted to prominence in the 1950s because of her play *A Raisin in the Sun*, and she went on to write a number of very outstanding and stellar works before prematurely passing away at the age of 34, in 1965.

I'm speaking of Claudia Jones[7] whose roots were in Trinidad, in the former West Indies. She joined the Communist Party at an early age and she was the leading activist in the Communist Party in Harlem, before running afoul of the authorities and being deported. She winds up in London where she, in the 1950s, becomes a leader of the growing Pan-Caribbean community that takes root in London, in the 1950s, and becomes the

---

experience and her struggles as an African-American woman.

4 See note on Paul Robeson on page 167

5 McCarthyism refers to a period of intense anti-communist suspicion and persecution in the United States during the late 1940s and early 1950s. The term derives from the name of Senator Joseph McCarthy, a Republican from Wisconsin, who played a prominent role in leading the anti-communist crusade at the time.

6 Lorraine Hansberry (1930-1965) was a playwright, writer, and activist. *A Raisin in the Sun* was the first play written by an African-American woman to be produced on Broadway.

7 Claudia Jones (1915-1964) was born in Trinidad. Jones migrated to the United States with her family in 1924. In the early 1950s, Jones faced political persecution during the McCarthy era. She was arrested and imprisoned for her communist activities, and in 1955, was deported from the U.S. She settled in London, England,. There is a chapter on Jones in Volume 1 of *Some Of Us Are Brave*.

founder and editor of the *West Indian Gazette*, a prominent journal of that time.

So, Shirley Graham Du Bois was not alone, in terms of her political radicalism. Was not alone in terms of her activism. But, having said that, I think it's still important to note that she was one of the most important Black women radical intellectuals of this, or any other, era.

TC: That was marvelous. Thank you oh so much ... *Race Woman: The Lives of Shirley Graham Du Bois.* Published by the New York University Press. So what is it that the younger generation can take away? Why is it important for the young generation of Black women, and Black men, to know about Shirley Graham Du Bois?

GH: Well, I think it's because of two things: One, her political activism. We don't have enough political activists today, to put it mildly. We don't have enough people who join organizations, who go to meetings, who take minutes at meetings, go door-to-door recruiting other members for the organization. That basic tradition of organizing has been lost, and she exemplifies that lost tradition.

We should also know about her because of her writing, particularly her political writing. Her writing that reflects radicalism. We don't have enough radical writers today. I think that that kind of tradition also is worthy of emulation.

TC: I'm speaking with Dr. Gerald Horne, Professor of History and African American Studies at the University of Houston. He's the author of so many books, but in particular, *Race Woman: The Lives of Shirley Graham Du Bois,* published by New York University Press. Dr. Horne, thank you so much for your time today.

GH: Thank you for inviting me.

Robin Kelley on Charlotta Bass

Robin DG Kelley is currently the Gary B. Nash Professor of History at UCLA. He is the author of numerous books including Hammer and Hoe: Alabama Communists During the Great Depression *and* Freedom Dreams: The Black Radical Imagination. *This audio was recorded at the Electric Lodge in Venice, CA, at a staged reading of Kia Corthron's "Live! From This Candidate" on Charlotta Bass's 1952 Presidential run on the Progressive ticket, performed by LisaGay Hamilton, October 2008. It was a fundraiser for the Southern California Library for Social Studies and Research. The Library is a local repository of progressive and radical history.*

• • •

Robin Kelley: I'm here for two reasons. Number one, to support the library. I have been dealing with this library since I was a college student at Long Beach State, in the early 1980s, so I have a 20-plus-year relationship with the library. Secondly, to hear LisaGay read this incredible play which is timely, challenging, and quite radical in many ways And hopefully, this is something that's just the beginning for what could be an interesting one-woman show going around the country, reminding us that change is something that you have to struggle for at the grassroots, and it's not something that you expect the President to bring to you. But that's why I'm here.

Thandisizwe Chimurenga: Now, you're currently teaching a class. I believe it's Black Radical Social Movements?

RK: It's called Black Movements in the U.S. Yeah.

TC: At USC. And I'm wondering, does Charlotta Bass figure in your coursework?

RK: She figures very prominently. I had all my undergraduates use the Southern California Library and their job was to basically pick somebody or some movement and to build a website using the Wikipedia or Wiki software. And so we have the central site at USC. I had at least three groups of students work on Charlotta Bass. So if you can go on the web right now and find these incredible websites. One focuses on Charlotta Bass and Garveyism, another focuses on Charlotta Bass and *The California Eagle*, and the third looks at the larger trajectory of political activism in the Progressive Party and before that. And so what we're gonna try to do is combine all three and make one big website. But the idea is to use the web, allow them to be multimedia, allow them to include music, words, other kinds of visuals, audio materials, rather than just write a paper. And so they learn a lot about Charlotta Bass, and she's a central figure in that project.

TC: Thank you so much for your time. Greatly appreciate your work.

RK: Thank you.

Yusef Omowale on Charlotta Bass

Yusef Omowale is the executive director of the Southern California Library for Social Studies and Research. The Library is a local repository of progressive and radical history. This audio was recorded at the Electric Lodge in Venice, CA, at a staged reading of Kia Corthron's "Live! From This Candidate" on Charlotta Bass's 1952 Presidential run on the Progressive ticket, performed by LisaGay Hamilton, October 2008. It was a fundraiser for the Southern California Library for Social Studies and Research.

• • •

Thandisizwe Chimurenga: Thank you for giving me your time. I greatly appreciate it. I appreciate the presentation that you made before the start of the reading, talking about your tenure here at the library. Congratulations, it looks like you've created some milestones in the midst of overcoming several hurdles. So congratulations.

Yusef Omowale: Thank you for that. Yeah, part of what I was saying is I've overcome some stuff, but really the library community is what helped do that. And that's what I think. A lot of people put their hope in Obama as a person ... the real hope is in what we do. And that's the point I was trying to make. And that's how the library still survives, is that folks have stepped up and made it happen.

TC: In your presentation, you talked a little bit about Charlotta Bass also and the fact that she does not have a headstone, she's in an unmarked grave, which I did not even know. That really bothered me.

YO: Yeah, me too. And I think that's symbolic of our history and the people that stand up for their rights, fight oppression. And that's a very physical metaphor for what's going on and the importance of the library to make sure that those kinds of stories are documented. But really part of my point too is that we've become a monument for people like Charlotta Bass. Not to put up on a pedestal, but the way in which we remember her and that we live, the things that she was trying to do is what becomes her marker.

TC: Now, I also thought it was very very poignant and compelling when you stated, and I'm hoping that you repeat for me also, you said that "You know it's bad when they demonize you by calling you by your name, Black, woman, radical, communist." Give me that again? I was like DAMN!

YO: Well, you just said it. Part of our demand is to call us by our true names. Right? Calling us by our true names means allowing for all of our history, who we are. And so when you go in a classroom, they don't wanna teach you about who you are. They're not letting you call yourself by your true name. And what's deep to me when I start thinking about it is that the way they demonize us is by actually describing who we are. So by the very fact, they called her Black, they called her woman, they called her all the things that she was trying to do as a way to silence her, and that's when she ended up having to sell her paper because they called her communist. I don't necessarily know that she was a communist, but that wasn't the point. They were calling her out for her radical ways, trying to fight the oppression that she saw during the day, and that's what they demonized her with. And that's what started tripping me out, too. And so some of the ways you see that we reclaim terms that have been used to demonize us. So that's why I was talking about how Black boys refer to each other in the terms of endearment, they reclaim the terms that people have used to demonize them and they make it their own.

TC: The Southern California Library is currently the repository of the Charlotta Bass papers and back issues of the *California Eagle*. Is that available for anyone to come in and view?

YO: That's what the library's about. That's available for anybody. That's our history, so we're able to look at it. You go to other archives, you have to show an ID, you have to get a letter of recommendation to be allowed to do research. Our library's a people's library, that's what we have.

The other thing about her marker and not having a gravestone, we have a photo collection for the *California Eagle*. One of the richest photographic archival collections of Black LA from that period. A lot of those, someone found those at a garage sale. That's the kind of stuff that would not be here if it wasn't for the people that built the Southern California Library and helped document the things that are in there today.

TC: So these are photographs from the *California Eagle*, and they ended up in someone's garage sale. Someone purchased them and brought them to the library?

YO: Exactly. And that's how we've got a lot of stuff we've had, is that someone's gonna throw stuff out into the trash and then someone – you know, we've literally gone and picked up things, from someone who's passed away, we've gone to the house and just emptied the stuff in trash bags, since the family's gonna throw everything away. And it's very important. It's our local history that we need to preserve. And so that's the kind of things that we have at the library.

TC: Are there any plans to, for example with Charlotta Bass: she has an autobiography that you can view at the library, you can read at the library, but it's out of print. Are there any plans to publish any of Charlotta Bass's writing? Are there any plans to reprint, republish her autobiography?

YO: We would like to do that, and we're looking into that now in terms of if we have the rights to do that. So that's something we're definitely trying to do. There's only a few copies of her memoir in existence. Stanford wanted to purchase one from us because they're very rare and hard to find. You come to the library, you're able to look at it yourself.

TC: Thank you so much, Yusef Omowale, for your time.

YO: Thank you for your support.

Editor's note: *Charlotta Bass is buried with her husband, Joseph Bass, in Evergreen Cemetery in East Los Angeles. Only Joseph's name appears on the headstone.*

Sistas in Struggle

Linda Evans on Anti-Imperialism

Linda Evans is a formerly incarcerated anti-imperialist human rights activist who served 16 years of a 40-year federal prison sentence for actions against the U.S. government. She is a founding member of All Of Us Or None, an organization that works to end discrimination against people with felony convictions, and she works with the California Coalition for Women Prisoners. Recorded at Mills College in Oakland, CA on February 10, 2005, and aired on WRFG 89.3-FM in Atlanta sometime in 2005 or 2006.

• • •

I'm glad to be here tonight. Thank you, everybody, for coming and for inviting us, and for a wonderful occasion to launch *Global Lockdown*, Julia's book.[1] I have to tell you that Black History Month has extra special memories for me because I did so many Black History months in prison. And we did a lot, you know? We did as many different kinds of celebrations as we could think of, during the time when there was a Black Cultural Workshop allowed, which was a prisoner organization. We would have big extravaganzas and plays and, you know, I always had to be either the slave catcher or John Brown,[2] which I kind of like being John Brown ... [laughter] ... that was a little closer to home for me. But I really appreciate

---
1 *Global Lockdown: Race, Gender and the Prison-Industrial Complex* edited by Julia Sudbury
2 John Brown (1800-1859) was an American abolitionist leader. Brown first gained attention when he led anti-slavery volunteers during the Bleeding Kansas Crisis of the late 1850s, a state-level civil war over whether Kansas would enter the Union as a slave state or a free state. He was eventually captured and executed for the failed incitement of a slave rebellion preceding the American Civil War.

Black History Month, and I am glad there's some other white people here to celebrate because I feel like it's a month for all of us, and that I in my own education, growing up in Iowa, you know many years ago, I'm pretty old now. We had no Black History, we had no history of other peoples. We had no Indigenous history, no Latino history. And I had to really fight and struggle in my own education to learn anything. So I really appreciate the fact that we're here today to celebrate Black History Month.

Julia asked me to say how I came to be in the book. And what I remember [laughter] is that shortly after I got out of prison, which now is four years ago. I was released by President Clinton on his last day in office which, as you know, was the same day that George Bush was inaugurated. I thought there was karma attached to me getting out and him being inaugurated as President, so I've tried to do my best to fight against his regime during the time that he's been President, and here we are, again. Shortly after I got out though, I was in the Critical Resistance office and I remember coming in and weeping. It's hard to come out of prison, I had left all my friends, I had left many of my comrades behind who were political prisoners also. And coming out, I felt like looking around me at the homelessness, at the suffering on the streets, at the economic degradation of our communities, of what people have to face, mostly when they come out of prison. I kind of felt like, we hadn't made a difference, and in the time that I had spent in prison, things had gotten worse. And I think that's true. I don't think it's the fact that we failed. I think it's a long struggle. But I went into prison originally for political actions against the U.S. government, basically trying to overthrow the government. And we didn't succeed in that, did you notice? [laughter]

But I walked into the Critical Resistance office, and I broke down crying, because Julia was there being her compassionate, generous self. And in the middle of this onslaught of tears, she says, "Linda, would you write an article for my book?" [laughter] Of course, I said, yes, I would do anything Julia asked me to do. And that's how I ended up writing this essay called "Playing Global Cop."

I don't think today I might use the word playing. I think that's perhaps a mistitle. But it's, you know, already published, so we can't change it now.

Do people know what anti-imperialist means? You know, it's a word that I think has great meaning today. But not everybody understands it.

So I kind of avoid that language without explaining it. Because I think what the United States is doing today is building empire. And it's just as clear today as it was during the war in Vietnam, or the whole history of the U.S. government. And there are so many incidents upon incidents upon incidents, but I feel that if we look at that as incidents, we miss the continuum that started when native people were thrown off their land and killed in genocidal attacks, and continued through slavery bringing Black people here from Africa, and the war on Mexico, you know, you could name them all. It's one system. And by calling myself an anti-imperialist, what I am trying to say is that we need to look at that history as a continuum. And not just as opposing the war in Iraq, or opposing the war in Vietnam, or even opposing racism here because there is a war on people of color here in this country, as we know. So I hope that we can begin to put the content back in what it means to be an anti-imperialist, and what it means to build anti-imperialist resistance without it being rhetoric.

There is real political meaning to empire. And it's really scary. Because I think that it's more important now than ever, that we develop an analysis about what's going on that can push us through, resisting the war in Iraq, or Afghanistan, or Colombia, or the Philippines, to developing an analysis that will allow us to build a revolutionary resistance to this government.

And while I was in prison, I finished my bachelor's degree. I dropped out of school early when I was your age, and became an activist, fighting against the war in Vietnam and developing that anti-imperialism that has sustained me through my life. A lot of it was because of the Black Studies, the movement for Black Studies. The first place that I became an activist was sitting down in an all-night sit-in at the administration building of Michigan State University, demanding Black professors and a Black Studies department and open admissions which, now, people don't even know what open admissions is. Does anybody in here know what it is? Open admissions? The old people [laughter]. Open admissions in Michigan, at Michigan State at that time, meant that anybody who passed out of high school got to go into college. It was a state university, everybody had the right to a college education. And now, of course, we know that tuition is so high at our state institutions that very few people can afford to go. There is no more affirmative action. So Black people, Indigenous people, Latino people are being shut out of the state universities. And open admissions is something that has disappeared. But one of the things that motivated me to begin to develop a political consciousness was the struggle of Black students at Michigan State.

And I moved from that to a field trip to Detroit where I walked on broken glass in the inner city around Wayne State, and struggled with exactly what your President [of Mills College] was talking about. How does the academy or college relate to the real world? And at that point, there was a growing student movement, and I decided, well, I can't relate to the "ivory tower." I'm going to join in the "school of life," so I dropped out, and eventually did finish my college education while I was in prison. And I also finished my master's degree while I was inside, because I was driven to understand what imperialism had developed into, and how it had changed during that 16 years that I was locked up. And what I began to understand was about globalization, and how the United States has manipulated and changed the ways, the multitude of ways, that it dominates the world. So that's part of what I wrote about in my essay. And I'll just read a tiny bit of it, because you guys can read for yourself.

Since the onset of the economic restructuring that we now know as globalization, communities of color in the United States have experienced increasing repression. The Nixon years introduced the war on crime, outlined in Nixon's 1973 State of the Union address. Please note, there are footnotes [laughter] which was a struggle. Reagan dramatically increased spending on policing and prisons through the intensification of the war on drugs. Both the war on crime and the war on drugs scapegoated and targeted poor communities of color. In many ways, these wars were preemptive strikes. As economic conditions deteriorate the strategy for social control is to put poor people away before they pose a serious threat to social order. The goal is to incarcerate and immobilize people oppressed by these social conditions, those at the bottom, the helpless, the hopeless, before they organize to demand change. Communities of color that are already ravaged by drug addiction, poverty and related violence have been further decimated by the war on drugs and mass imprisonment.

So when I got out of prison, after 16 years I, along with Stormy[3] and George [Galvis], and others, co-founded an organization called All Of Us or None. Basically, what we're fighting for, is to build a movement of people who have been in prison, whose families had been in prison, who have gone through the criminal justice system, had felony convictions, maybe didn't go to prison, but have been ravaged by mass imprisonment. Because we recognize that it's not just the individuals, it's not just Stormy as an individual woman, or me as an individual woman, or George as a young person who went to prison. It's our whole communities that are affected by the prison industrial complex, and by the millions of people – almost six million people now – are under the jurisdiction of the criminal justice system in this country.

Ten million children have parents who have been in prison. What does that do? What kind of scars does that leave on families and communities? That's what we have to fight back against. And that's the movement that we're trying to build with All Of Us or None. I brought some literature here. It's on that table back there. This is a brochure. This is a briefing packet, you know, we're trying to make changes in public policy. And it's hard for me to swallow to tell you the truth, because I never thought that I would be involved in reforming the system. But it's a matter of survival. It's really a matter of survival at this point. The demands that we're making as All Of Us or None, are six:

Number one, that all the cities and counties in the Bay Area and hopefully eventually statewide, prohibit all forms of discrimination against people that are based on our past criminal histories. That means ban that box from the employment applications, from the housing applications, from the student aid applications, and the welfare applications. There are so many types of discrimination that people face once they've gone to prison, once they've had any kind of contact with the criminal justice system. You go to county jail for a night, you're gonna lose your job, you could possibly lose your house, your whole family might get evicted if you get convicted of a drug felony. You know, it goes on and on. And I talked about that in my essay also.

Our second demand is to end the welfare ban. In California, as well as 20 other states in the United States, if you are convicted of a drug felony,

---

3 See next chapter.

you never again can get Temporary Aid to Needy families [TANF], which is CalWorks here. Never again. If you have a drug felony that is not simple possession, you can't get food stamps. What does that mean for women? Getting out of prison? How do you have any kind of resources to reunite your families, feed your children? So we want California to opt out of the federally-imposed welfare ban.

Our third demand, shut down CYA. And we've made really good strides toward doing that, you know? There have been some victories. There was a court settlement that said that the California Youth Authority must be changed so that it now will be regional, kids will be closer to their families. It's still not good enough, we want to shut it down. My niece, and I'm white middle class. My niece was in CYA for almost four years now. And while she was inside she was molested sexually by the guards. Six guards. And she's bringing a lawsuit along with some of the other girls in CYA that suffered the same kind of abuse. But it's rampant. I mean, probably some of you saw the beatings, you know, of the young men that were on TV. This is commonplace, we were just lucky that Gloria Romero[4] put that tape out into the public so that people could actually see it. So it's not a struggle that's over, we need to continue to put pressure on them to shut it down and allow the children to be in group homes in alternative situations where they can stay with family members, and have programs so that they actually have something to live for, besides violence, and abuse.

Our fourth demand is that the Bill of Rights for Children of Incarcerated Parents should be adopted. I don't know if it's in here, you know, there's a series of rights that children themselves wrote. And I think it's very, very important that we support the demands of young people who have suffered just as much as their parents, from the incarceration of whole families.

Our fifth demand is to ban that box on all the applications for public employment. And we're introducing, actually a resolution in front of the Human Rights Commission of San Francisco to do exactly that. And we hope to be able to do it here in the East Bay, in San Mateo County, and eventually statewide.

---

4 California State Sen. Gloria Romero. "Videotape of Beating by CYA Officers Is Released," *Los Angeles Times*, April 2, 2004.

And our sixth demand is to increase reentry services that are community-based. And I want to be clear with everybody, you know? There's a lot of talk "Oh those prisoners, they come out all they want is, you know, more services." There aren't services. Almost 80% of the people coming out of prison end up homeless. That same percentage ends up unemployed. And it really isn't, doesn't require rocket science to understand why the recidivism rate of people going back to prison is 67 percent in California. They can't get jobs, you can't get a house to live in. What else are you going to do to feed your family or be with your family? What are your choices, you know? So, as long as there is discrimination, there will never be enough services, because we don't have an equal chance. And that's what we're trying to end in All Of Us or None.

There are lots and lots of ways that all of you can help, whatever your relationship has been to the criminal justice system. One thing is get rid of Jerry Brown,[5] do not elect him as Attorney General. He is pushing hard for a curfew against all people on parole and probation so that people coming out of prison are going to stay in prison, but there'll be locked up in house arrest from 10 at night to 6 in the morning. But what if you want to go to a late movie, or what if you want to go to visit your family or to an AA meeting at midnight which a lot of people in recovery do? Or maybe you want to go jogging at five o'clock in the morning before you go look for work.

One of the most important things, and one of the most difficult things for me coming out of prison was to learn to make decisions. We visit jail sometimes and do outreach in jail. And I swear, it puts me right back in that same place of going up to a door and just standing there. Because I know it's locked. I can't open that door. Of course, it's not. But that's a prison thing. In prison, you never have a key, you never can open a door. And that mentality lasts a long time.

It's difficult to make decisions when you come out of prison, even about the maybe simplest things. So to rob people of the ability to make a decision about staying up past 10:30 at night is something that is not going to contribute

---

5 Edmund Gerald Brown Jr. (1938-) is an American lawyer, author, and politician who served as the 34th and 39th governor of California from 1975 to 1983 and 2011 to 2019. A member of the Democratic Party, he was elected Secretary of State of California in 1970. He later served as Mayor of Oakland from 1999 to 2007 and Attorney General of California from 2007 to 2011.

to reducing crime in Oakland. So we need your support to end the curfew. We need your support to stop discrimination against people. We need to make sure that the universities don't have that box on their applications for entrance, which some of them do. And I think that what that means is that we need to build a movement, a politically powerful movement that links the issue of prisons with the survival of our communities, and especially communities of color because there is a war on.

And I remember very well, when I was an agitator against the Ku Klux Klan[6] in Texas and trying to exhort people, you know, just push people with the power of my own passion to take action against the Klan. I used to talk about the war against Black people and the war against Indian people. And in Texas, that's who the Klan was making war against. And it's still true. Maybe the Klan is parading in suits. Maybe the Klan used to be liberal, like Jerry Brown. But they're alive and well. And white supremacy is alive and well. And it's all of our responsibility, especially the white people, to fight against it. And that's got to be part of the consciousness that we bring to the political movement that we build, wherever we're active.

What is the war in Iraq about? Well, yeah, it's white supremacy. There's no doubt of that. It's Christian supremacy, no doubt about it. So I think it's really important for us to analyze what's going on, to be clear about the continuum so we can push our movement ideologically. And push it in terms of a strategic approach to changing it and ending the system and building it to be extremely powerful so that we can eventually win, because we need to win.

---

6   See note on the Ku Klux Klan on page 14.

Stormy Ogden on Native American Women

Stormy Ogden is Kashaya Pomo from Stewart Point and a recognized member of the Tule River Yokuts tribe. She is a prison rights activist who has worked with the American Indian Movement for several years. While serving a five-year sentence at the California Rehabilitation Center at Norco, Stormy campaigned for the first sweat lodge to be built in a women's prison.

Recorded at Mills College in Oakland, CA on February 10, 2005, and aired on WRFG 89.3-FM in Atlanta sometime in 2005 or 2006.

• • •

I'd like to introduce myself again. I'm Stormy Ogden, I'm Tule River Yokuts tribe. The Yokuts tribe is my grandmother's tribe. And at one time we occupied the whole San Joaquin Valley. My grandpa's people is Kashaya Pomo. And that is from Stewart's Point, which is coastal area. I was told that when we come and talk to people, that we need to introduce who our family members are, who our tribal people are. And I'd also like to welcome all the other indigenous people that are sitting in this audience tonight, whether you be indigenous of these lands, indigenous of the Mexico area, indigenous of Africa, indigenous of wherever, I'd like to welcome you here tonight.

I wasn't real sure how I wanted to start and how I wanted to do this. And Julia said, maybe I should talk about how I got to be part of this book. So I was thinking about that, and I thought, okay, well, I should tell you guys a story. And I know some of you have heard this story before, but I'm going to tell it again. Because this introduces how I got to be part of this project.

My grandfather's people, like I said, is Kashaya Pomo. And they say that if you give a child a live cricket, that the child will eat that cricket, and it makes their voice strong, so they can sing all night. And it makes it clear so the dancers can hear the song because our ceremonies are done at night, and they're done to the dancing. Well, I have these two cats and this was about four years ago when I first met Julia. And this one cat, which decided that it was going to be my baby, started bringing in crickets, which I thought was a little peculiar because his brother was bringing in mice and birds and rodents, right? What a cat should be bringing in. But Igmoo, my cat, was bringing in these live crickets dropping them at my feet. Well, I called my cousin up and was telling my cousin about this. And he said, "Well, somebody, the Creator, is telling you that your voice needs to be strong. So you can speak for the women. So you can speak for the Indian women, the indigenous women, the native women."

And that was the same time I was asked to speak at the first Incite! Conference.[1] And that was down in Santa Cruz. And that was the first time I met Julia Sudbury. And I tell you that story because Julia Sudbury has become another cricket for me, she has helped me get my voice to be as strong as it is, as powerful as it is, as clear as it is. And I'm honored to know Julia, I'm honored to be part of this because Julia has always been there for me as far as bringing up issues of native women, of native people, because we're always forgotten about. You always hear about the other groups, but you never hear that much about indigenous people, native people. So that's how I got to be here, that's how I got to write this article. And I'm honored, Julia. I'm so honored to be part of this. I'm a little bit nervous and I'm excited about it. This is the second time that I've ever been published. But to be part of Julia's book is extra special to me, because she's always been there. She's my cricket.

[Laughter]

I don't know what to read. I really want to tell you all to buy the book. But I guess maybe just a little bits and pieces?

"I write this chapter from the position of a California Indian woman, a tribal woman of Yokuts and Pomo ancestry. I also write as an ex-prisoner and

---

1 "The Color of Violence: Violence Against Women of Color," was a conference held at the University of California-Santa Cruz on April 28-29, 2000. Out of this conference came the organization INCITE! Women of Color Against Violence.

a survivor of colonialism. At the beginning of the colonialism process two tools of genocide were forced upon the native people: the bottle and the bible. Along with these tools, the traditional ways of behavior and conduct of native people were criminalized. State and federal governments defined Native Americans as deviant and criminal through such procedures as the Dawes Act. With the enforcement of these new laws, native people were locked up in a series of punishing institutions including military forts, missions, reservations, boarding schools, and most recently state and federal prisons.

"The little girl who grew up to be a convict." All of my women role models were white. They did not know how to deal with this Indian child who grew so dark in the summer. During the school year they would cut and perm that "Injun" hair, putting me in pretty dresses and telling me in soft, hushed voices, "Your dad is just a dirty drunk Indian and you will be just like him." In my house, I laid upon strange beds in a motel praying that I would not wake up in the morning. At these times, it was done as a ritual; long hot showers purifying my body, combing my long dark hair, wrapping it into neat braids, singing my own death songs. Other times I would be sitting on the side of an empty bed, around me would be empty whiskey bottles, and a shiny new razor blade in my hand."

One of the things that I found when I was in prison is that we no longer were considered humans, we were no longer considered women, we were no longer considered native people. You're listed through classification as being Black, white, Mexican, or other. Native people were listed as others. Outside the door of our dorm, where I was at, they would have my name, they would have my state number, and they would put "other" on it. Well, every morning I would get up and go to my state paid job and I would take down the word "other" I'd cross it out and I put American Indian. So this went on for about a week or so and the guard told me if I did it one more time that I was going to lose time behind it. Well, the next morning I got up and I was late for my state job because I had to find a permanent laundry marker. And I ripped the tag off of the wall and put "Stormy Ogden Kashaya Pomo and Tule River Yokuts." I got sixty extra days for it. But it was worth it.

"Just as alcoholism has touched the life of every Native person, so has the United States criminal justice system, in particular the prison system.

As Luana Ross points out, most native people have been incarcerated themselves or have a relative who was in prison." You don't have to raise your hands but just think about it, how many people in here know a family member that is doing time or has done time?

"The outcome of this high rate of imprisonment can be only described as genocidal. The native world has been devastated by foreign laws that were forced upon them, and the number of jailed natives is a chilling reminder of that fact. Native people are being locked up at an alarming number in our own ancestral lands. For the Indigenous women of North America sexual assault and imprisonment are two interlocking, violent, colonial mechanisms. The criminalization and imprisonment of native women can be interpreted as yet another attempt to control indigenous lands and as part of the ongoing effort to deny native sovereignty." Right now, California has the highest population of women in prison. And native women are the highest population because we're like 1% of the population in all, but we have the highest rate of people of native people in prison. And we're still forgotten about. We're still never brought up. We're still never thought about. We're still never talked about. When you talk about the prison industrial complex, who's been talked about? Latinos, African-Americans. Well where are the indigenous people? Where are the native peoples of these lands? This is still Indian land. Not one single treaty was ever kept. We were not given one single treaty to have things come to us. So this is still Indian land.

Linda and I were talking about some of the things that happened to us while we were in prison. And I was talking about how dehumanizing it is. I was down at California Institute for Women and I was being brought back up to county for another charge. And I believe I was in Merced or Modesto. And at that time I was state property. Well, when they put me in the county jail to transfer me up, they couldn't decide if I was state or if I was county property. So they didn't know what color jumpsuit to put me in. So they threw me into the holding cell naked for most of the night, and there were only male guards there. The whole time I was there I was given elavil, mellaril, thorazine and chloral hydrate because I was a native woman, because I was an alcoholic, because I had addiction to drugs. And this happens to a lot of the women in there. My sister was put into prison about six years ago. She was in Stockton for about four years. She was afraid to go to counselors and talk about what was going on with her. She had two children at home, she had an alcoholism problem, she had a drug addiction problem. She was afraid to go and talk to the counselors because she was afraid that they were going to medicate her.

Now, I walked around in what's known as the "Thorazine Shuffle" because I didn't know what was happening. And to this day, I still have ramifications from all those psych drugs that were given to me. I had one very close sister. She was a Dineh, a Navajo woman. And we lost her on the prison grounds. Nobody could find her. She was in the chapel, underneath one of the pews, all rolled up in a ball because they had given her so much medication because she thought spiders were coming and getting her. And instead of taking her to the hospital, they took and put her in rack for 90 days. So she withdraw from the medication and then being in rack, which is like being in isolation, which means she had no clothes, she had no blankets, she had no mattress, she had nothing. And this is happening to our women today continuously. And it's a cycle that's happening within all of our families, about our people being locked up.

In my family, my grandfather died in San Quentin. I was the first child of my dad's to go to prison. My brother was after me, and then my sister was after me. So half of my dad's kids ended up in prison. We ended up in prison behind drugs and alcoholism, mainly alcoholism for me. But I became an activist. After prison I became an activist, an advocate as soon as I was born a native woman, because I'm always preaching for our rights. For those of you who have had the pleasure of having Julia as an instructor, I applaud you. Listen to what she has to say. She's very wise. She's got strengths that I couldn't even begin to talk about. She's very passionate about this. And like I said, I'm happy to be part of this. Hopefully, I'll be going to the next Incite! Conference to speak again.

In closing, I'd like to say, what was my crime? Why five years in prison? Less than $2,000 for welfare fraud. What was my crime? Being a survivor of molestation and rape. What was my crime? Being addicted to alcohol and drugs. What was my crime? Being a survivor of domestic violence. What was my crime? Being an American Indian woman.

Mitakuye Oyasin
[All My Relations]

About The Author

Thandisizwe Chimurenga is an award-winning freelance journalist based in Los Angeles, CA. She is a former Assistant Editor of the LA-Watts *Times* newspaper and a former reporter and co-anchor for Free Speech Radio News and the KPFK Evening News (Pacifica). She has been a commentator for *Hard Knock Radio*, a daily public affairs show for the Hip-Hop generation heard on KPFA Radio (Pacifica-Berkeley) and has been recognized as a "Champion of National News Reporting" by the San Francisco *BayView* Newspaper, Block Report Radio and the County of San Francisco, as well as New America Media for "Outstanding Reporting on Health and Health Care."

A writer and creator or co-creator of grassroots community media (newspapers, cable TV, radio) for over 20 years, she co-founded *Some of Us Are Brave: A Black Women's Radio Program* with others in 2003.

Her activism has ranged from electoral organizing; anti-police terror work; freedom for political prisoners and prisoners of war; to organizing against violence against women. Her first book, *No Doubt: The Murder(s) of Oscar Grant*, was independently published in 2014.

She is currently the host of *Rootwork: Getting Down to the Roots*, a show of analysis, news and interviews airing on KPFK and the Black Power Media platform.